KNIT WITH BEADS

Stunning Shawls & Wraps

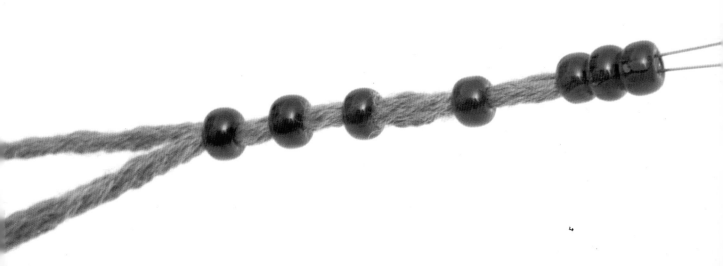

KNIT WITH BEADS

Stunning Shawls & Wraps

Easy Techniques • 15 Beautiful Designs

Scarlet Taylor

Photographs by Donald Scott

WATSON-GUPTILL PUBLICATIONS
NEW YORK

SENIOR ACQUISITIONS EDITOR: JOY AQUILINO
EDITOR: PATRICIA FOGARTY
ART DIRECTOR: JULIE DUQUET
DESIGNER: LISA HAMILTON
SENIOR PRODUCTION MANAGER: ALYN EVANS
PHOTOGRAPHER: DONALD SCOTT

First published in 2007 by Watson-Guptill Publications,
Nielsen Business Media, a division of The Nielsen Company
770 Broadway, New York, NY 10003
www.watsonguptill.com

ISBN-10: 0-8230-1675-7
ISBN-13: 978-0-8230-1675-4

Library of Congress Control Number: 2006936854

Manufactured in China

First printing, 2007

1 2 3 4 5 6 7 8 9 / 15 14 13 12 11 10 09 08 07

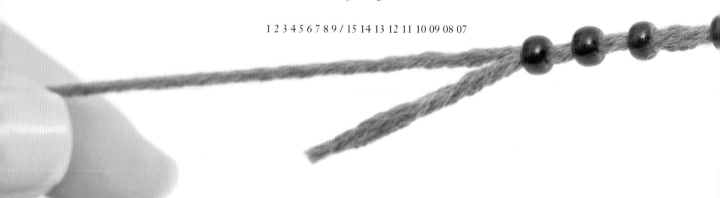

DEDICATION AND ACKNOWLEDGMENTS

*T*his book is dedicated to my oldest daughter, Coy Taylor, who, as my deadline quickly approaches, is about to "leave home" for the first time for her freshman year of college, beginning a new and exciting venture in her life . . . just like Mom.

I'd like to express my deepest gratitude to Melissa Leapman, without whose encouragement and support I would never have taken on this project. I consider myself fortunate to have her as a mentor, and especially blessed to call her friend.

A special thank you to the following talented knitters for their hard work, dedication, and enthusiasm in creating the stunning garments for this book: Bobbi Anderson, Stella Bedard, Mary Elliott, Leah Galliker, Sheila Jones, Andrea Kelly, Maureen McGuiness, Marci (Posey) Salem, and Eleanor Swogger.

Thanks to the talented staff at Edge of Urge in Wilmington, North Carolina, for their great sense of styling, and for providing wardrobe items for the models.

Thanks to Leah Williams for the use of her charming home for photography and as our "base camp" during the shoot. And for keeping us going with her great coffee!

Thanks to Jay Gartrell at Blue Heaven Bed & Breakfast in Wilmington, North Carolina, for his "southern hospitality" and for graciously allowing us the use of his lovely inn for photography.

Thanks to Gina Allison and her staff at Caravan Beads in Wilmington, North Carolina, for their enthusiasm and inspiration, for allowing me to come into the store and "try on" beads, and for sharing their vast knowledge of beads with me.

Thanks to Donald Scott for the beautiful photography, and for his willingness to allow me to "make it mine." Thanks to our lovely and very patient models Cari, Kelly, Mary, and Morgan. And to Danna for hair and makeup that stood up to the test of not only our summer heat and humidity, but a tropical storm as well!

Thanks to Charlotte Quiggle for her thoroughness in editing these patterns, and for her endurance during her sickness to see this project completed.

Thanks to my editor, Joy Aquilino, for this incredible opportunity, and for her support and enthusiasm.

My sincere gratitude to my project editor, Patricia Fogarty, and copy editor, Andrea Curley, for their efforts in making this book a success.

Thanks to graphic artist Natalie Fuechsel for her work on the charts and schematics.

And most importantly, to my incredible family, Phillip, Coy, and Katie: Your endless support of my work is inspiring to me every day, and doesn't go unappreciated. To my husband, Phillip, who made sure that Coy's applications for college were actually submitted on time. And that Katie's sixteenth birthday was special, even during a hectic photo shoot. To Coy and Katie, who try so hard not to complain about eating dinner at 9:00 p.m. Thank you so much for everything you do for me.

CONTENTS

INTRODUCTION *9*

CHAPTER 1 *Stringing It All Together* *10*

Bead Basics 10

Beads and Knitting Yarns 10

Pre-Stringing Beads 12

Blocking and Laundering 14

Casting on Stitches with Beads 13

Things You Should Know 14

CHAPTER 2 *Knitting with Beads in Garter Stitch* *15*

Fireside Shawl 16

Double-Breasted Cape with Beaded Trim 20

Sassy Shrug 24

CHAPTER 3 *Knitting with Beads Between Purl Stitches* *28*

Beaded Tweed Poncho 30

Southwestern Poncho 34

CHAPTER 4 *Slip-Stitch Beaded Knitting* *38*

Pearl Capelet 40

Enchanted Shawl 44

Nautical Shrug 48

CHAPTER 5 *Knitting with Beads Through a Stitch* 52

Argyle Wrap   54

Sapphire Dream Capelet   58

CHAPTER 6 *Knitting with Beads on a Yarn-over* 62

Spring Morn Shawl   64

CHAPTER 7 *Hook Beading* 68

Bows and Beads Ponchini   70

Bobbles and Beads Capelet   74

CHAPTER 8 *Stitching Beads to Knitted Fabric* 78

Houndstooth Stole   80

CHAPTER 9 *Knitting with Sequins* 84

Shimmering Shawlette   86

GLOSSARY OF TERMS AND TECHNIQUES 90

KNITTING ABBREVIATIONS 94

SOURCES FOR MATERIALS 95

BIBLIOGRAPHY 96

INDEX 96

INTRODUCTION

$\mathcal{F}$or those of us who have this passion, this *need to knit* in our lives, it seems only natural to want to lovingly embellish the beautiful fabric we create. While others may accent with fine embroidered stitchery or appliqué with creative fabric shapes, my interest has been ignited by beads: shiny, glittery, and polished beads, warm, iridescent, and vibrant beads. Whether small or large, beads can be worked into nearly any knitted design, adding texture and color to the simple stitchwork of a scarf or hat, fringed to accent the hem of a skirt or capelet, scattered across a sweater, or grouped into a distinct color pattern or shape.

Knit with Beads: Stunning Shawls and Wraps provides basic instructions and illustrations for several creative techniques of knitting and embellishing with beads.

Each chapter presents a different "knitting with beads" technique, along with easy and fun-to-knit projects for you to learn from. And don't worry! You don't have to buy, strand, and knit thousands of beads to add a little *bling* to your projects. The stylish and fashionable wraps presented in the following pages were designed with some of your favorite yarns, in beautiful colors and easy-to-knit stitch patterns. So, get beading! It's easier than you think.

CHAPTER 1
Stringing It All Together

Bead Basics

There are hundreds of sizes and shapes of beads made from beautiful materials such as glass, wood, stone, clay, metals, gemstones, plastic, and more. Some are lined with color, painted, or dyed. Just visit a local bead store or online supplier and you'll find more choices than you could possibly imagine. With all the fun and easy techniques for knitting with beads, you are sure to find a way to add your favorites to almost any knitting project.

Many of the designs in this book use glass seed beads. They are by far the easiest beads to find and use for the majority of your knitting projects. And the colors are gorgeous. Seed beads come in sizes ranging from very tiny 15/0 and 11/0 (used for stitching beads to knitted fabric—see page 78) to larger 6/0 or 5/0, sometimes referred to as "E" beads. The larger the number the smaller the bead. Pebble beads are yet a little larger.

The key factor when choosing beads to use in knitting projects is the size of the center hole. It must be large enough for the bead-stringing needle to pass through with a double thickness of the yarn. A good rule of thumb is to think 6 and 6: a size 6/0 bead is a good choice for a medium-weight yarn (DK to worsted weight) or a yarn that suggests a size 6 needle. All beads are not created equal. Japanese seed beads typically have larger holes than Czech beads and are typically more uniform in size. If you try to substitute a Czech bead for a Japanese bead, make sure before you begin that it's large enough to thread on the yarn.

Beads and Knitting Yarns

When choosing yarns and beads to knit with, keep a few considerations in mind for successful results. Make sure that the bead is a good match for your yarn. You wouldn't want to use a very delicate bead on a garment or purse that will receive a lot of wear and tear. When using lined beads, bear in mind that the color can sometimes wear or rub off from excessive stress when pre-stringing. Also be mindful of the fiber content of your yarn. I used a bone bead for the Spring Morn Shawl (page 64) to go with Green Mountain Spinnery's Cotton Comfort, a yarn spun from organic cotton and wool. The organic nature of the bone bead made it a perfect choice!

Each of the projects in this book was designed with a specific yarn and bead in mind. Unique characteristics that make up the yarn—such as fiber content, twist, and weight—were taken into consideration in my choice of the right bead. Then I chose a beading technique that would best contribute to the success of the project. For best results, I recommend that you use the yarn suggested in the pattern.

If you need to make a yarn substitution, be sure to follow the suggestions made above for choosing beads and yarns. If possible, before purchasing beads, try them on the yarn you prefer for a good fit. As with any knitting project, take the time to knit a swatch in the pattern stitch. Use whatever needle size you need to obtain the specified gauge.

Pre-Stringing Beads

There are beading needles and beading threads made specifically for beading purposes. For pre-stringing beads, I like to use a "big-eye" needle.

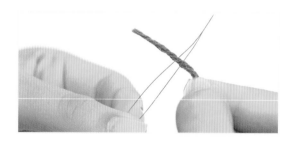

1 The big-eye needle is made up of very thin, flexible wire that separates at the center, forming the "eye." Thread the yarn through the eye (left) and secure at one end, leaving a short tail.

2 Thread each bead onto the needle at the opposite end, pushing the beads down the needle, then down the yarn (above). Tip: Don't try to thread too many beads at once; if there's a bead with a smaller hole that won't fit, you'll have to remove all the beads to discard it.

3 To prevent excessive wear on the yarn, unwind a generous length of yarn from your ball and push the beads down in small groups. Wind the yarn back into a ball, leaving a few beads close to the end so that they are available as you need them (above).

Where a pattern instructs you to pre-string beads, the number of beads given is the approximate number necessary for working the bead pattern while knitting with the first ball of yarn. If you find you need a few more beads as you near the end of the ball, don't cut your yarn—simply thread the additional beads from the tail end. If you have a few beads left over, just slide them off the yarn. Thread each additional ball of yarn with beads as needed to complete the pattern.

The total number of beads given in the materials list for each project is the approximate number of beads needed to complete the entire project—plus a few more to compensate for beads that are unusable. Often when you buy beads there will be some that are either broken or that have holes that are not completely drilled out. Just discard those beads, or save them for other projects where they can be used.

Casting on Stitches with Beads

Adding beads to your cast-on creates the most beautiful cast-on edge. Use this technique for the beaded rosette in the Pearl Capelet pattern (page 40) and the lovely scalloped edge in the Sapphire Dream Capelet pattern (page 58).

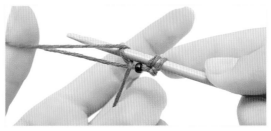

1 *You'll need to use the long-tail cast-on (see the Glossary for an explanation and illustrations). Unwind enough yarn to cast on the given number of stitches for your project. Pre-string and slide the beads down the strand so that they are on the "tail" coming from the skein. Make a slip knot and place it on the needle, then cast on 1 more stitch (you'll have 2 stitches on the needle, as above).*

2 **Slip 1 bead up close to the needle (above), then cast on 2 stitches (more if you would like your beads to be farther apart). Repeat from * until you have 1 fewer stitch than needed, then cast on the last stitch.*

Things You Should Know

Instructions for many of the knitting techniques you'll need to complete the projects can be found in the Glossary of Terms and Techniques (page 90). The Knitting Abbreviations list (page 94) includes standard knitting abbreviations as well as special ones used in this book. Instructions given for the beading techniques are for knitting flat (back and forth in rows) unless otherwise stated.

Blocking and Laundering

For knitted fabrics with beads, it's best to use a wet blocking technique, as most beads will not hold up well to steam or direct heat from pressing with an iron. I've found that lightly spraying the finished piece with cool water, blotting out the excess water with a clean white towel, then pinning the piece on a blocking surface to dry works very well.

Extra care should be taken in laundering your beaded knits. It's best to hand-wash the garment as you would your other delicate hand knits, taking special care of the beads. You may want to ask your bead stockist for advice on laundering specific types of beads you are purchasing. If the yarn label suggests dry cleaning, be sure to advise your dry cleaner not to steam or otherwise stress the beads.

Skill Levels

The skill levels described for each project in this book reflect the standards provided by the Craft Yarn Council of America:

Beginner Projects using basic knit and purl stitches, for first-time knitters. Minimal shaping is involved.

Easy These projects use basic stitches, repetitive stitch patterns, and simple color changes, and involve simple shaping and finishing.

Intermediate Projects that use a variety of stitches, such as basic cables and lace, simple intarsia, double-pointed needles, and knitting-in-the-round needle techniques, with mid-level shaping and finishing.

Experienced These projects can involve intricate stitch patterns, techniques, and dimension, such as non-repeating patterns, multicolored techniques, fine threads, small hooks, detailed shaping, and refined finishing.

CHAPTER 2
Knitting with Beads in Garter Stitch

$\mathscr{T}$his is the easiest of all techniques for knitting with beads. And it's fun!

Although beads are added to Garter stitch on a wrong-side (WS) row, the beads fall to the right side (RS) of your work. All you need to do is slide a bead up close to your needle, then knit the next stitch. The bead will sit in front of and between two stitches. Watch your tension to make sure that the bead stays firmly in place against the fabric. You don't want it to be "droopy" or so tight that the fabric puckers.

In the charts for patterns using this technique (that is, where the bead sits between two stitches), the bead is drawn on the vertical line in the graph between two stitch squares. You should work the first stitch as indicated in the chart (in this case, knit), slide the bead up, then work the next stitch as indicated (also knit when working Garter stitch).

TECHNIQUE

With pre-strung yarn, knit across the row to the desired bead position indicated in the pattern or chart by SBU. Keep the yarn at the back (WS) of your work in knit position, slide one bead up close to the needle, then knit the next stitch as usual (above). The bead then sits on the strand between two knit stitches on the right side. Make sure the bead doesn't "droop" on the strand. It should rest nicely against the fabric.

Sample fabric knit with beads in Garter stitch.

FiresideShawl

This is a great "first project" for learning to knit with beads using an easy technique. If you're a little uncomfortable with the knitting skills required for some of the other projects, not to worry—this pattern was designed for the beginner knitter. The pattern is basic Garter stitch with a simple yarn-over (yo) increase. If you're not familiar with the yarn-over, check the Knitting Abbreviations list on page 94 for instructions.

Knitters of any experience level will love working with this "to die for" yarn. It's the perfect background for these warm, bronze beads. Bring on winter!

SKILL LEVEL Beginner

SIZE One size

APPROXIMATE FINISHED MEASUREMENTS
Width at top edge: 72"
Length: 42"

MATERIALS
- Artful Yarns *Portrait* (70% mohair / 25% viscose / 5% polyester, 164 yds/150m, 1.75 oz/50g): 8 skeins #161 Nude with a Hat
- Approx 900 size 6/0 Glass Japanese Seed Beads (sample knit with #16221, from Wichelt Imports/Mill Hill Beads)
- Size 10 (6mm) knitting needles, or size needed to obtain gauge
- Bead-stringing needle
- Tapestry needle
- Crochet hook for fringe

GAUGE
In Garter st, 14 sts and 24 rows = 4"/10cm.
To save time, take time to check gauge.

PATTERN STITCHES
GARTER STITCH
Knit every row.

BEAD PATTERN (MULT 6 STS + 6)
Bead Row: K3, SBU, *k6, SBU; rep from *, ending k3.

SPECIAL ABBREVIATION
SBU = Slide 1 bead up to the RH needle into position indicated in pat.

Instructions

Pre-string approx 130 beads.

Cast on 4 sts.

Knit 1 row.

Set Up Patterns
Next Row (RS): K1, yo, k2, yo, k1—6 sts.

Next Row: K3, SBU, k3.

Shawl Shaping
Row 1 (RS): K1, yo, knit to last st, yo, k1—8 sts.

Row 2: Knit.

Rep Rows 1 and 2 for shawl shaping AND AT SAME TIME work Bead Pat Row on following 4th row once, then every 6th row 39 times—248 sts.

Knit 2 rows even.

Bind off.

Finishing
Weave in loose yarn ends.

Fringe
See the Glossary for general instructions for Simple Fringe (page 93). For this project, cut 328 strands of yarn, each 8" long, for 82 fringes.

For each fringe, fold 4 strands in half, insert crochet hook from back to front through stitch, and pull fold through to back. Pull ends through fold and secure.

Evenly fringe along each side of center point. Trim neatly to desired length.

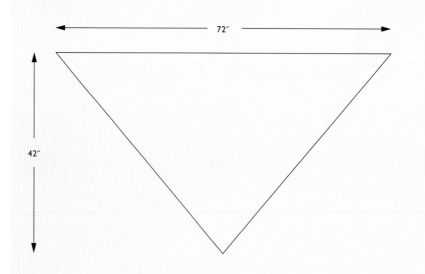

Double-BreastedCape

WITH BEADED TRIM

This project is an example of how combining just the right yarn with just the right bead can fashion the style for a garment. I started with a yarn—Donegal Tweed Homespun wool—that would be perfect for a classic double-breasted style, then searched for a complementary bead and found these dark wooden ones. Used for the trims, they add just enough interest and a natural feel to this sophisticated cape.

SKILL LEVEL Intermediate

SIZES S (M, L, XL). Instructions are for smallest size, with changes for other sizes noted in parentheses as necessary.

FINISHED MEASUREMENTS (Double-breasted with overlap buttoned)
Circumference at lower edge: 52 (55½, 60, 64½)"
Circumference at shoulder: 44½ (48, 52½, 57)"
Length: 18½ (18½, 19, 20)"

MATERIALS

- Tahki Yarns *Donegal Tweed Homespun* (100% pure new wool, 183 yds/169m, 3.5 oz/100g): 5 (6, 7, 8) skeins #804 Grape
- Approx 370 (385, 400, 425) 5mm round brown wooden beads
- Size 6 (4.25mm) straight and 29" circular needles
- Size 8 (5mm) 24" and 29" circular needles, or size needed to obtain gauge
- Bead-stringing needle
- Three stitch holders
- Two stitch markers
- Tapestry needle
- Six 1" buttons (sample shows JHB International's Leather-All Brown, style #60335)

GAUGE

With larger needles in St st, 18 sts and 24 rows = 4"/10cm.
To save time, take time to check gauge.

PATTERN STITCHES

BEADED CAPE BORDER (MULT OF 4 STS + 1)
See Beaded Cape Border chart, or in words:
Row 1 (WS): *K1, SBU, k3; rep from * to last st, k1.
Row 2 and all RS rows: Knit.
Row 3: *K3, SBU, k1; rep from * to last st, k1.
Row 5: Rep Row 1.
Row 7: Rep Row 3.
Row 8: Knit.

STOCKINETTE STITCH (ST ST)
Knit on RS rows, purl on WS rows.

GARTER STITCH
Knit every row.

SPECIAL ABBREVIATION

SBU = Slide 1 bead up to the RH needle into position indicated in pat.

Instructions

Pre-string approx 264 (280, 300, 320) beads. With smaller circular needle, cast on 265 (281, 301, 321) sts.

Work Rows 1–8 of Beaded Cape Border from chart, or instructions at left. Change to larger circular needle and beg with WS row work 3 rows in St st.

Buttonhole Row (RS): K3, bind off 3, k20, bind off 3, knit to end of row (see Pattern Notes). Rep Buttonhole Row every 38 (38, 40, 44) rows twice more.

Work even in St st until piece measures approx 5" from beg, ending with a WS row.

Begin Shaping

Dec Row 1 (RS): K42 (45, 45, 45), k2tog [k16 (17, 19, 21), k2tog] 10 times, k41 (44, 44, 44)—254 (270, 290, 310) sts. Work even until piece measures approx 9" from beg, ending with a WS row.

Dec Row 2 (RS): K41 (44, 44, 44), k2tog, [k15 (16, 18, 20), k2tog] 10 times, k41 (44, 44, 44)—243 (259, 279, 299) sts. Work even until piece measures approx 13" from beg, ending with a WS row.

Dec Row 3 (RS): K41 (44, 44, 44), k2tog [k14 (15, 17, 19), k2tog] 10 times, k40 (43, 43, 43) sts—232 (248, 268, 288) sts. Work even until piece measures approx 13½ (13½, 14, 15)" from beg, ending with a WS row. On last row, pm after first 66 (70, 75, 80) sts and before last 66 (70, 75, 80) sts.

Pattern Notes

- *Circular needles are used to accommodate the large number of sts. Work the cape and the collar back and forth in rows, changing lengths when necessary.*
- *To make buttonholes, work to buttonhole position, bind off 3 sts. On following row, cast on 3 sts over bound-off sts.*

Shape Shoulders and Neck

Dec Row (RS): Knit to 2 sts before first marker, skp, slip marker, k2tog; knit to 2 sts before next marker, skp, slip marker, k2tog; knit to end row—2 sts dec'd each shoulder.

Rep Dec Row every other row 12 (9, 10, 10) times more, then every row 0 (4, 3, 3) times **AND AT SAME TIME,** when piece measures approx 15½ (15½, 16, 17)" from beg, ending with a WS row, **SHAPE NECK:** Bind off 22 sts at beg of next two rows for neck edges. Bind off 4 sts at each neck edge once, then bind off 2 sts at each neck edge once.

Dec Row (RS): K1, ssk, knit to last 3 sts (and cont working shoulder decs), end k2tog, k1—1 st dec'd at each neck edge. Rep Dec Row every other row 3 times more. Complete shoulder decs—116 (128, 148, 168) sts.

Divide and Bind Off for Shoulders

Right Front

Next Row (RS): K21 (24, 29, 34) sts for right front, turn. Put rem sts on separate needle for holder.

Bind off 7 (8, 10, 11) sts at beg of next 2 WS rows for shoulder, then bind off rem 7 (8, 9, 12) sts.

Back

With RS facing, slip next 74 (80, 90, 100) sts to working needle for back; join yarn. Bind off 7 (8, 10, 11) sts at beg of next 4 rows, then bind off 7 (8, 9, 12) sts at beg of next 2 rows. Slip rem 32 sts to holder for back neck, cut yarn.

Left Front

With RS facing, slip rem 21 (24, 29, 34) sts to working needle for left front; join yarn. Bind off 7 (8, 10, 11) sts at beg of next 2 RS rows, then bind off rem 7 (8, 9, 12) sts on last RS row.

Finishing

Sew bound-off shoulder edges together.

Front Bands

With RS facing and smaller needle, pick up and knit 65 (65, 67, 72) sts evenly along left front edge. Knit 1 row. Bind off loosely knitwise. Rep for right front edge.

Collar

With RS facing and smaller needle, beg and end approx 5¼" from front edges, pick up and knit 78 sts evenly around neck edge including sts from holder. Work in Garter st for approx 3½", ending with a RS row.

Cut yarn, and pre-string 78 beads. Join yarn and work Beaded Cape Collar pat from chart, or in words:

Row 1 (WS): *K1, SBU, k3; rep from * to last 2 sts, k1, SBU, k1.

Row 2 and all RS rows: Knit.

Row 3: *K3, SBU, k1; rep from * to last 2 sts, k2.

Row 5: Rep Row 1.

Row 7: Rep Row 3.

Bind off loosely.

With RS facing and smaller needle, pick up and knit 20 sts along right front neck edge between front edge and collar. Knit 1 row. Bind off loosely knitwise. Rep for left front neck edge.

Sew buttons to correspond to buttonholes. Weave in loose yarn ends.

BEADED CAPE BORDER

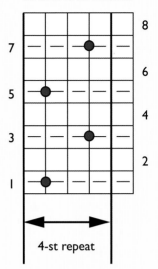

4-st repeat

BEADED CAPE COLLAR

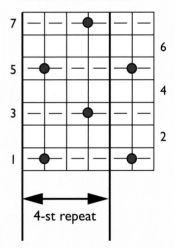

4-st repeat

KEY

☐ = Knit on RS, purl on WS

⊟ = Purl on RS, knit on WS

⊡ = SBU between 2 knit stitches

18½ (18½, 19, 20)″

7″

3″

5″

7″ OVERLAP

13½ (13½, 14, 15)″

44½ (48, 52½, 57)″

52 (55½, 60, 64½)″

SassyShrug

When you are thinking about adding beads to your knitting, sometimes you need look no further than the simple design details you're already familiar with, such as these picots. What a perfect place for a bead! Because both Picot Cast-on and Picot Bind-off are worked from the wrong side, we can use the technique for Knitting with Beads in Garter Stitch (page 15) to add a bead to a sassy little picot point.

SKILL LEVEL Easy

SIZES S (M, L). Instructions are for smallest size, with changes for other sizes noted in parentheses as necessary.

FINISHED MEASUREMENTS
Center back to cuff: 30 (31¼, 32½)"
Length from back neck to bottom edge: 13½ (15¼, 17½)"
Length from cuff to cuff: 60 (62½, 65)"

MATERIALS

- Moda-Dea *Sassy Stripes* (100% acrylic, 147 yds/135m, 1.75 oz/50g): 5 (7, 8) skeins #6946 Crush
- Approx 125 size 6/0 Czech E-Beads (sample knit with #25199-12 Hematite Iridescent, from A Touch of Glass)
- Size 4 (3.5mm) knitting needles
- Size 6 (4.25mm) knitting needles, or size needed to obtain gauge
- Four stitch markers
- Bead-stringing needle
- Tapestry needle

GAUGE
With larger needles in St st, 22 sts and 32 rows = 4"/10cm.
With smaller needles in Beaded Picot Cast-on and Beaded Picot Bind-off, 22 sts = 4"/10cm.
To save time, take time to check gauge.

PATTERN STITCHES

BEADED PICOT CAST-ON (MULT OF 4 STS + 6)
With smaller needles, using knit-on cast-on technique (see Glossary), *cast on 6 sts, k2 sts, bind off first st, SBU, k1, bind off 1 st (2 sts bound off), slip rem st from RH needle to LH needle; rep from * until 2 sts rem to be cast on, cast on 2 sts.

BEADED PICOT BIND-OFF FOR SLEEVE (MULT OF 4 STS + 6)
Bind off first 2 sts, *sl st on RH needle to LH needle, using knit-on cast-on technique, cast on 2 sts, k2, bind off first st, SBU, k1, bind off 5 sts; rep from * across.

STOCKINETTE STITCH (ST ST)
Knit on RS rows, purl on WS rows.

GARTER STITCH
Knit every row.

SPECIAL ABBREVIATION
SBU = Slide 1 bead up to the RH needle into position indicated in pat.

Instructions

Pre-string 12 (13, 14) beads.

With smaller knitting needles, using Beaded Picot Cast-on, cast on 50 (54, 58) sts.

Work in Garter st for approx 1", ending with a RS row.

Change to larger needles, and beg St st. Inc 1 st (M1) each edge every 8th row 2 (2, 16) times, then every 10th row 0 (11, 3) times, then every 12th row 7 (2, 0) times, then every 14th row 3 (0, 0) times—74 (84, 96) sts.

Cont even until piece measures approx 19¾ (20¾, 21¾)" from beg, and pm to indicate end of first sleeve.

Work even until piece measures approx 40¼ (41¾, 43¼)" from beg, and pm each side to indicate beg of second sleeve.

Work even for approx 1" from marker, ending with a WS row.

Pattern Notes

- *Shrug is a shaped rectangle, knit from cuff to cuff.*
- *To work incs for first sleeve shaping: RS Rows: K2, M1, knit to last 2 sts, M1, k2.*
- *To work decs for second sleeve shaping: RS Rows: K2, ssk, knit to last 4 sts, k2tog, k2.*

Dec 1 st each edge on next row, then every 14th row 3 (0, 0) times, then every 12th row 7 (2, 0) times, then every 10th row 0 (11, 3) times, then every 8th row 1 (1, 15) times—50 (54, 58) sts.

Cont even until second sleeve measures approx 18¾ (19¾, 20¾)" from marker, ending with a WS row; pm each side. Shrug should measure approx 59 (61½, 64)" from beg.

Change to smaller needles, and work even in Garter st for approx 1", ending with a RS row. Cut yarn.

Pre-string 12 (13, 14) beads.

Bind off, using Beaded Picot Bind-off.

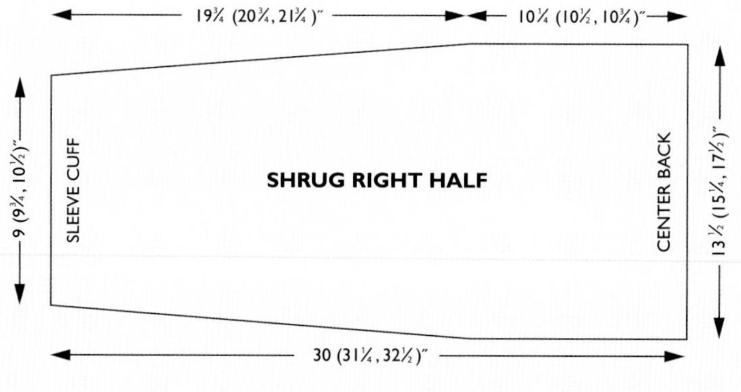

19¾ (20¾, 21¾)"
10¼ (10½, 10¾)"
9 (9¾, 10½)"
SLEEVE CUFF
SHRUG RIGHT HALF
CENTER BACK
13½ (15¼, 17½)"
30 (31¼, 32½)"

Finishing

Fold rectangle in half lengthwise. Beg at cuff edge, sew sleeve seam approx 19¾ (20¾, 21¾)" to markers. Rep at opposite end for second sleeve. This leaves an opening in the center of the shrug for shoulders and body. Adjust sleeve lengths if necessary.

Beaded Picot Band

Pre-string 37 (38, 39) beads.

With RS facing and smaller needles, pick up and knit 116 (119, 122) sts along one long edge of shrug beg and ending at underarm edge of sleeve seam. Work even in Garter st for approx 1", ending with a RS row.

Next Row: Work Beaded Picot Border as follows:

Bind off first 2 sts, *sl st on RH needle to LH needle, using knit-on cast-on technique, cast on 2 sts, k2, bind off first st, SBU, k1, bind off 4 sts; rep from * across.

Rep for second side. Sew band sides together at underarm. Weave in loose yarn ends.

CHAPTER 3
Knitting with Beads Between Purl Stitches

*I*f you can purl, you can knit with beads using this technique. It's that easy.

With this technique, the bead sits on the strand and is held in place between two purl stitches on either side. You'll want to make sure that the strand isn't too loose or the bead will look "droopy" and be prone to snagging. On the other hand, you don't want to pull too tightly either, because that will cause the fabric to pucker under the bead. Practice on your gauge swatch, and you'll get it in no time at all.

In the charts for patterns using this technique (that is, where the bead sits between two purl stitches), the bead is drawn on the vertical line in the graph between two stitch squares. You should work the first stitch as indicated in the chart (in this case, purl), slide the bead up, then work the next stitch as indicated (also purl).

TECHNIQUE

1 *With pre-strung yarn, work across the right-side (RS) row to within one stitch of the desired bead position indicated in the pattern or chart by SBU. Purl the next stitch (above).*

2 *Then with the yarn still in front of your work, slide one bead up close to the needle and purl the next stitch. The bead then sits on the strand and is held in place between two purl stitches on the right side (above). Make sure the bead doesn't "droop" on the strand. It should rest nicely against the fabric.*

Sample fabric knit with beads between purl stitches.

This technique is not only easy, it's a great way to add interesting texture to your fabric.

For even more interest, I've used mixed beads for this project to create a tweed effect on a solid color yarn. To best achieve this effect, place the beads randomly as you knit to mimic your favorite tweed yarn. Or refer to our model photograph as a guide.

Have some fun as you string the differently colored beads. Make your own pattern of colors (remember to string the beads in reverse order of how you want them placed on the fabric), or just let the beads fall where they may. Think of it as sprinkling flecks of color all over your fabric.

SKILL LEVEL Easy

SIZE One size

FINISHED MEASUREMENTS
Circumference at lower edge: 68"
Circumference at shoulder: 40"
Length: 22½"

MATERIALS
• Reynolds *Utopia* (100% acrylic, 225 yds/206m, 3.5 oz/100g): 5 skeins #73 brown
• Approx 1400 size 6/0 Japanese Seed Beads (sample knit with #6-Mix-19 Good Earth, from Caravan Beads)
• Size 6 (4.25mm) knitting needles
• Size 8 (5mm) circular needle, or size needed to obtain gauge
• Cable needle
• Bead-stringing needle
• Two stitch markers
• Tapestry needle

GAUGE
With larger needles in St st, 18 sts and 26 rows = 4"/10cm.
With larger needles, 17-st Four-Rib Braid Cable = 2½"/6.35cm.
To save time, take time to check gauge.

PATTERN STITCHES
FOUR-RIB BRAID CABLE (17-ST PANEL)
See chart, or in words:
Row 1 (WS): [K2, p2] twice, k1, [p2, k2] twice.
Row 2: P2, k2, p2, sl next 3 sts to cn and hold in back, k2, sl the purl st from cn back to LH needle and purl it, then k2 from cn, p2, k2, p2.
Row 3: Same as Row 1.
Row 4: P2, *sl next 2 sts to cn and hold in front, p1, k2 from cn, sl next st to cn and hold in back, k2, p1 from cn, p1; rep from * once more, end p1.
Row 5: [K3, p4] twice, k3.
Row 6: P3, sl next 2 sts to cn and hold in back, k2, k2 from cn, p3, sl next 2 sts to cn and hold in front, k2, k2 from cn, p3.
Row 7: Same as Row 5.
Row 8: P2, *sl next st to cn and hold in back, k2, p1 from cn, sl next 2 sts to cn and hold in front, p1, k2 from cn, p1; rep from * to last st, end p1.
Row 9: Same as Row 1.
Row 10: P2, k2, p2, sl next 3 sts to cn and

hold in front, k2, sl the purl st from cn to LH needle and purl it, k2 from cn, p2, k2, p2.
Rows 11–16: Rep Rows 3–8.
Rep Rows 1–16 for pat.

STOCKINETTE STITCH (ST ST)
Knit on RS rows, purl on WS rows.

GARTER STITCH
Knit every row.

K1, P1 RIB (ODD NUMBERS OF STS)
Row 1 (RS): *K1, p1; rep from * to last st, k1.
Row 2: *P1, k1; rep from * to last st, p1.
Rep Rows 1 and 2 for pat.

Instructions

Back
Pre-string approx 270 beads.

With smaller needles, cast on 159 sts.

Work in Garter st for approx 1", ending with a RS row.

Next Row (WS): Change to larger

needles, p71, pm, work Row 1 of Four-Rib Braid Cable across center 17 sts, pm, p71.

Cont working St st on sides and Cable pat as est between markers, and beg randomly placing beads to achieve desired tweed effect. Work 6 rows even.

Next Row (dec) (RS): Knit to 4 sts before first marker, ssk twice, slip marker, work cable pat, slip marker, k2tog twice, knit to end of row—155 sts.

Cont in pats as est, and rep Dec row

every 8th row 7 times, then every 6th row 8 times—95 sts. Piece should measure approx 18½". Rep Dec row every 4th row 4 times, then every other row 4 times—63 sts. Piece should measure approx 22½".

Work 3 rows even**, removing markers.

Next Row (RS): K5, k2tog, [k1, k2tog] 17 times, k5—45 sts rem.

Neckband
Change to smaller needles, and beg with Row 2, work in K1, P1 Rib pat until band measures approx 3½" from beg, ending with a WS row. Bind off loosely in rib.

Front
Work same as for Back to **, but do not remove markers.

Next Row (RS): K5, [k2tog, k1] 6 times, work Cable pat between markers, [k1, k2tog] 6 times, k5—51 sts rem.

Neckband
Next Row (WS): Change to smaller needles, and beg with Row 2, work K1, P1 Rib pat across first 17 sts, work Cable pat between markers, work K1, P1 Rib pat across rem 17 sts.

Cont in pats as est until band measures approx 3½", ending with Row 3 of Cable pat. Bind off loosely in pat.

Finishing
Sew side seams, including neckband.

Weave in loose yarn ends.

4 RIB BRAID CABLE

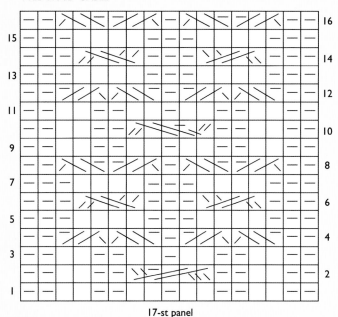

17-st panel

KEY

▢ = Knit on RS, purl on WS

▬ = Purl on RS, knit on WS

= Slip 3 sts to cn and hold in back, k2, slip the purl st from the cn back to left needle and purl it, then k2 from cn

= Slip 2 sts to cn and hold in front, pl, k2 from cn. Slip next st to cn and hold in back, k2, pl from cn

= Slip 1 st to cn and hold in back, k2, pl from cn. Slip next 2 sts to cn and hold in front, pl, k2 from cn

= Slip 2 sts to cn and hold in back, k2, k2 from cn

= Slip 2 sts to cn and hold in front, k2, k2 from cn

= Slip 3 sts to cn and hold in front, k2, slip the purl st from the cn back to left needle and purl it, then K2 from cn

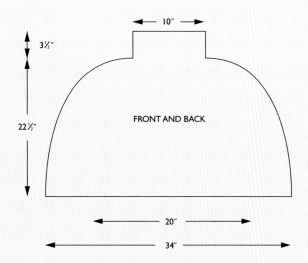

FRONT AND BACK

10″

3½″

22½″

20″

34″

SouthwesternPoncho

Beads can be used to create geometric patterns and motifs. Try working a favorite Fair Isle pattern, with colored beads rather than colored yarns. Or, using one of the techniques in this book, design your own.

Start by charting out the design on graph paper so that you can "see" each stitch necessary, not only to create the design but also to work the chosen beading technique. For example, this southwestern motif is made using the Knitting with Beads Between Purl Stitches technique (page 28). Therefore you need two stitches, one on either side, to add a bead.

SKILL LEVEL Easy

SIZES (S/M (L). Instructions are for smallest size, with changes for other sizes noted in parentheses as necessary.

FINISHED MEASUREMENTS
Width (including borders): 35½ (41¼)"
Length from shoulder: 22½"

MATERIALS
- Patons *Classic Wool* (100% wool, 3.5 oz/100g, 223 yds/204m):
  - 1 (1) ball #206 Russett (A)
  - 1 (1) ball #220 Bottle Green (B)
  - 1 (2) ball #215 Blue Storm (C)
  - 2 (3) balls #224 Grey Mix (D)
  - 2 (3) balls #207 Rich Red (E)
  - 1 (1) ball #77023 Camel (F)
- Approx 1625 (1900) size 6/0 Japanese Seed Beads (sample knit with #5 5636 Silver, from Beads World, Inc.)
- Size 5 (3.75mm) knitting needles
- Size 7 (4.5mm) knitting needles, or size needed to obtain gauge
- Size E-4 (3.5mm) crochet hook for neckband
- Bead-stringing needle
- Two stitch holders
- Tapestry needle

GAUGE
With larger needles in St st, 20 sts and 26 rows = 4"/10cm.
To save time, take time to check gauge.

PATTERN STITCHES
BEADED X'S AND ARROWS (MULT OF 28 STS)
See chart, or in words:
Row 1 (RS): Knit.
Row 2 and all WS Rows: Purl.
Row 3: K8, p1 SBU p1, k2, *k6, p1 SBU p1, k3, [p1 SBU] 3 times, p1, k2, [p1 SBU] 3 times, p1, k3, p1 SBU p1, k2; rep from * to last 16 sts, k6, p1 SBU p1, k8.
Row 5: K5, p1 SBU p2 SBU p1, k3, *k1, p1 SBU p1, k4, p1 SBU p2 SBU p1, [k2, p1 SBU p1] 2 times, k2, p1 SBU p2 SBU p1, k3; rep from * to last 16 sts, k1, p1 SBU p1, k4, p1 SBU p2 SBU p1, k5.
Row 7: K4, p1 SBU p2 SBU p1, k4, *p1 SBU p2 SBU p1, k4, p1 SBU p2 SBU p1, [k2, p1 SBU p2 SBU p1] 2 times, k4; rep from * to last 16 sts, [p1 SBU p2 SBU p1, k4] 2 times.
Row 9: K3, p1 SBU p2 SBU p1, k5, *k1, p1 SBU p1, k6, p1 SBU p2 SBU p1, k2, p1 SBU p1, k2, p1 SBU p2 SBU p1, k5; rep from * to last 16 sts, k1, p1 SBU p1, k6, p1 SBU p2 SBU p1, k3.
Row 11: K2, p1 SBU p2 SBU p2 SBU [p1 SBU] 3 times, p1, k1, *k5, [p1 SBU] 4 times, [p2 SBU] 2 times, p1, k4, p1 SBU [p2 SBU] 2 times, [p1 SBU] 3 times, p1, k1; rep from * to last 16 sts, k5, [p1 SBU] 4 times, [p2 SBU] 2 times, p1, k2.
Row 13: Work same as Row 9.
Row 15: Work same as Row 7.
Row 17: Work same as Row 5.
Row 19: Work same as Row 3.
Row 20: Purl.

STRIPE PATTERN FOR BOTTOM EDGE
2 rows each D, B, and A; 4 rows C; 2 rows each D and C; 4 rows each E, F, and D—26 rows.

STRIPE PATTERN FOR BODY (WORKED IN ST ST)
4 rows each D and B; 2 rows each C, F, and C; 4 rows E; 2 rows each D and A; 4 rows D; 2 rows each B, C, and A; 4 rows each F and D—40 rows.

STOCKINETTE STITCH (ST ST)
Knit on RS rows, purl on WS rows.

GARTER STITCH
Knit every row.

SPECIAL ABBREVIATION
SBU = Slide 1 bead up to the RH needle into position indicated in pat.

Instructions

Back
With smaller needles and D, cast on 168 (196) sts.

Beg 26-row Stripe Pat for Bottom Edge pat **AND AT SAME TIME** work in Garter st for approx 1" for bottom edge border.

Change to larger needles and St st. Cont in Stripe Pat for Bottom Edge as est, and work even until last row has been completed. Cut yarn.

With E, pre-string approx 398 (468) beads.

Join E and work Rows 1–20 of Beaded X's and Arrows pat from chart, or written-out row-by-row instructions.

Work 40-row Stripe Pat for Body. Cut yarn.

With E, pre-string approx 398 (468) beads.

Join E, and work Rows 1–20 of Beaded X's and Arrows pat.

Work even in Stripe Pat for Body until piece measures approx 21" from beg, ending with a WS row.

Divide for Neck Opening
Next Row (RS): Cont in Stripe Pat as est, k59 (73) sts, and place on a holder for right shoulder; loosely bind off center 50 sts for neck; k59 (73) sts for left shoulder.

Working on left shoulder sts only, cont even until last row of Stripe Pat has been completed (approx 1½"). Bind off.

Slip right shoulder sts back to needle and rejoin yarn to WS. Complete right shoulder same as for left shoulder.

Front
Work same as for Back.

Finishing
Sew shoulder seams.

Neck Edge
With WS facing, crochet hook, and D, work 2 rnds of single crochet around neck edge (see Glossary). Fasten off.

Side Borders

With RS facing, smaller needles, and D, pick up and knit 219 sts along left side (front and back) edge of poncho. Work in Garter st until band measures approx 1", ending with a WS row. Bind off. Rep for right-side edge.

Weave in loose yarn ends.

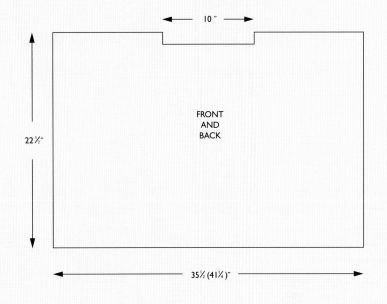

BEADED X'S AND ARROWS

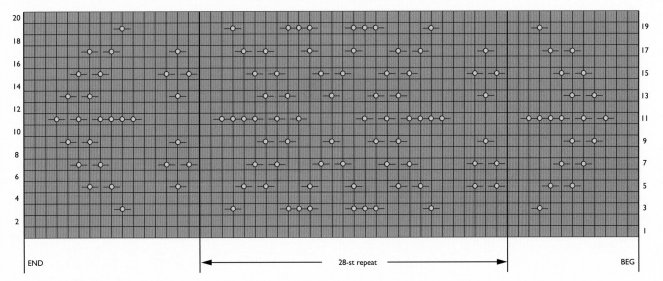

KEY

■ = Knit on RS, purl on WS

▭ = Purl on RS, knit on WS

⊕ = SBU between 2 purl stitches

CHAPTER 4
Slip-Stitch Beaded Knitting

*I*f you love slip-stitch knitting as much as I do, you'll really love this technique.

When you slip a stitch with the yarn in front of your work, you are left with that little strand of yarn that "floats" in front of the stitch that was slipped. What a perfect place for a bead . . . or two or three!

In slip-stitch beaded knitting, the beads are pre-strung, making it easy to slide a bead right up in front of a slipped stitch. You'll need to pay attention to your tension as you take the yarn back to the wrong side of your work and knit the next stitch. You want to be firm enough to hold the bead in place neatly, but you don't want the strand to be so tight that the fabric puckers.

TECHNIQUE

1 *With pre-strung yarn, work across the row to the desired bead position indicated in the pattern or chart by SBU. Bring the yarn forward to the right side (RS) of your work (wyif) between the two needles. Slip the next stitch (purlwise) from the left-hand needle to the right-hand needle (above).*

2 *Slide one bead up close to the right-hand needle, placing it in front of the slipped stitch. Keeping the bead in front (RS) of the work, bring the yarn to the back (WS) again to knit (above). Knit the next stitch as usual.*

Sample fabric knit with slip-stitch beaded knitting.

PearlCapelet

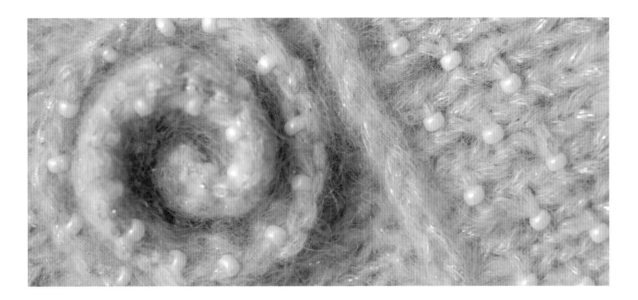

It's not often that you can use a novelty or bulky yarn when knitting with beads. The very characteristics that we love about novelties (fuzzy, bumpy, thick, and thin) can make stringing beads quite difficult. And bulky weight? No way a bead will fit. But here's an exception. This yarn is so soft that the strand easily flattens out as the beads are stranded. Voilà—knitting with beads on a bulky novelty yarn!

This is another pattern in which the beads have been used to accent an existing design detail—the ruffle. And the beaded rosette is simply beautiful and really easy to make.

SIZES S (M, L, XL). Instructions are for smallest size, with changes for other sizes noted in parentheses as necessary.

FINISHED MEASUREMENTS

Circumference at lower edge (excluding ruffle): 48½ (52¼, 56, 59¼)"
Circumference at shoulder: 35 (38¾, 45, 48½)"
Length: 17 (17½, 18, 18½)"

MATERIALS

- Red Heart *Bijou* (49% nylon / 25% kid mohair / 17% wool / 9% metallic, 84 yds/77m, 1.75oz/50g): 5 (6, 7, 8) skeins #3638 Peridot
- 420 (440, 460, 475) size 6/0 Japanese Seed Beads (sample knit with #6-591 Ivory Pearl Ceylon, from Caravan Beads)
- Size 11 (8mm) 29" and 24" circular needles, or size needed to obtain gauge
- Size 13 (9mm) knitting needles
- 11 (11, 9, 9) stitch markers
- Bead-stringing needle
- Tapestry needle
- Safety pin (for Beaded Rosette)

GAUGE

With smaller needles in St st, 13 sts and 18 rows = 4"/10cm.
To save time, take time to check gauge.

PATTERN STITCHES

BEAD PATTERN (MULT OF 4 STS + 2, DECREASED TO MULT OF 2 STS)
See Instructions.

STOCKINETTE STITCH (ST ST)
Knit on RS rows, purl on WS rows.

REVERSE STOCKINETTE STITCH (REV ST ST)
Purl on RS rows, knit on WS rows.

SPECIAL ABBREVIATION

SBU = Slide 1 bead up to the RH needle into position indicated in pat.

Instructions

Ruffle

With 29" circular needle, using the long-tail cast-on technique (see Glossary), cast on 314 (338, 362, 386) sts. Work in St st for 2½", ending with a WS row.

Cut yarn, and pre-string 234 (252, 270, 288) beads.

Work Ruffle Decrease Row and Begin Bead Pattern

Row 1 (RS): K1, *sl 1 wyif, SBU, k3tog; rep from * across, ending k1— 158 (170, 182, 194) sts.

Row 2: Purl.

Row 3: K1, *k1, sl 1 wyif, SBU; rep from * across, ending k1.

Pattern Note

Circular needles are used to accommodate the large number of sts. Work the Capelet back and forth in rows, changing lengths when necessary.

Row 4: Purl.

Row 5: K1, *sl 1 wyif, SBU, k1; rep from * across, ending k1.

Body

Work 7 rows in St st.

Dec Row (RS): K8 (9, 10, 12), pm, k2tog, [k12 (13, 18, 19), pm, k2tog] 10 (10, 8, 8) times, k8 (9, 10, 12)— 147 (159, 173, 185) sts.

Work 7 rows even.

K2tog after each marker this row,

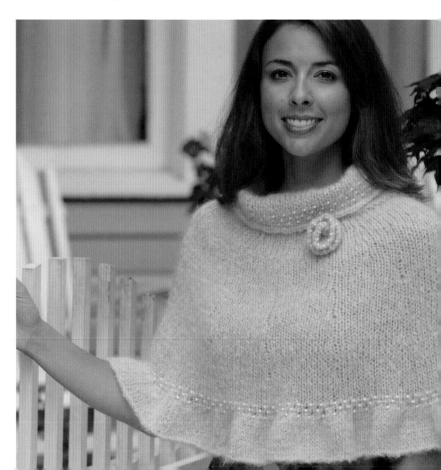

then every 8th row twice more—114 (126, 146, 158) sts. Remove markers.

Work even in St st until piece measures approx 12½ (13, 13½, 14)" from beg, ending with a WS row.

Decrease for Shoulder and Neck

Dec Row 1 (RS): K8 (8, 9, 5), k2tog, [k14 (10, 5, 5), k2tog] 6 (9, 18, 21) times, k8 (8, 9, 4)—107 (116, 127, 136) sts.

Work 5 rows even.

Dec Row 2 (RS): K8 (9, 10, 4), k2tog, [k8 (6, 5, 5), k2tog] 9 (12, 15, 18) times, k7 (9, 10, 4)—97 (103, 111, 117) sts.

Work 5 rows even.

Dec Row 3 (RS): K7 (9, 10, 4), k2tog, [k7 (5, 4, 4), k2tog] 9 (12, 15, 18) times, k7 (8, 9, 3)—87 (90, 95, 98) sts.

Work 5 rows even.

Dec Row 4 (RS): K8 (5, 2, 6), k2tog, [k5 (4, 3, 2), k2tog] 10 (13, 18, 21) times, k7 (5, 1, 6)—76 sts rem.

Collar

Next Row (WS): Knit. Cont in Rev St st as est, and work even until collar measures approx 3". Change to larger needles, and work even until collar measures approx 6", ending with a RS (purl) row.

Work Bead Pattern

Cut yarn, and pre-string approx 111 beads.

Row 1 (WS): K1, *k1, sl 1 wyif, SBU; rep from * across, ending k1.

Row 2: Purl.

Row 3: K1, *sl 1 wyif, SBU, k1; rep from * across, ending k1.

Row 4: Purl.

Row 5: Work same as Row 1.

Row 6: Purl.

Bind off very loosely.

Sew side seam from bottom edge to collar. Reverse seam, and cont to sew collar seam. Weave in loose yarn ends.

Beaded Rosette

Beaded Cast-on Edge

See "Casting on Stitches with Beads," on page 13. Unwind enough yarn from skein to cast on 48 sts using the long-tail cast-on technique (see Glossary) and pre-string 47 beads.

Slide beads down strand so that they are on the "tail" coming from the skein; with smaller knitting needles, make a slip knot on needle (first st). Cast on 1 st (2 sts on needle), *slide 1 bead up close to needle, then cast on 2 more sts. Rep from * until you have 48 sts on needle.

Rosette

Rows 1, 3, 5: Knit.

Row 2 (RS): K1, k2tog, *sl 1 wyif SBU, k2tog; rep from * to end—32 sts.

Row 4: K1, k2tog, *sl 1 wyif SBU, k2tog; rep from * to last 2 sts, sl 1 wyif SBU, k1—22 sts.

Row 6: K2tog across—11 sts.

Cut yarn and draw through rem sts. With RS facing, roll piece into rosette shape. Fasten off. Weave in loose yarn ends. Attach with safety pin to center front just below collar, or as desired.

23 ½"

7½"

4½"

FRONT & BACK

17 (17½, 18, 18½)"

12½ (13, 13½, 14)"

35 (38¾, 45, 48½)"

48½ (52¼, 56, 59¼)"

This is that one shawl you'll want to wear with everything. The yarn . . . the beads . . . the fringe—not only enchanted, but enchanting! The pattern combines two beading techniques. Use the Slip-Stitch Beaded Knitting technique (page 38) to knit the shawl. This creates the perfect "canvas" to which you can add your own personal touch by stitching on additional beads (see page 78 for a description of this technique).

SKILL LEVEL Beginner

SIZE One size

APPROXIMATE FINISHED MEASUREMENTS
Width: 24½"
Length: 64½" (excluding fringe)

MATERIALS
- Plymouth *Suri Merino* (55% suri alpaca / 45% extra fine merino wool, 110 yds/ 100m, 1.75 oz/50g): 15 skeins #2174 light blue
- Approx 275 size 6/0 White Ceylon Czech Seed Beads; 75 size 6/0 Lt. Sapphire S/L Rbw Matte Czech Seed Beads; 130 size 8/0 Crystal Czech Seed Beads; and 130 size 8/0 White Ceylon Czech Seed Beads (sample knit with #102 White Ceylon, #651 Lt. Sapphire, #100 Crystal, #102 White Ceylon, from The Bead Wrangler)
- Size 7 (4.5mm) 29" circular needle, or size needed to obtain gauge
- Two stitch markers
- Bead-stringing needle
- Beading needle
- Beading thread to match yarn and bead (white or light blue works best)
- Tapestry needle
- Crochet hook for fringe

GAUGE
In St st, 22 sts and 31 rows = 4"/10cm.
To save time, take time to check gauge.

PATTERN STITCHES
TRI-BEAD PATTERN (MULT OF 24 STS + 1)
Row 1 (RS): K13, [sl 1 wyif SBU, k1, sl 1 wyif SBU, k21] 4 times, sl 1 wyif SBU, k1, sl 1 wyif SBU, k13.
Row 2: Purl.
Row 3: K14, [sl 1 wyif SBU, k23] 4 times, sl 1 wyif SBU, k14.
Rows 4–34 (31 rows): Work in St st.
Row 35 (RS): K1, [sl 1 wyif SBU, k1, sl 1 wyif SBU, k21] 5 times, sl 1 wyif SBU, k1, sl 1 wyif SBU, k1.
Row 36: Purl.
Row 37: K2, [sl 1 wyif SBU, k23] 5 times, sl 1 wyif SBU, k2.
Rows 38–68 (31 rows): Work in St st.
Rep Rows 1–68 for pat.

STOCKINETTE STITCH (ST ST)
Knit on RS rows, purl on WS rows.

SEED STITCH (ODD NUMBER OF STS)
Row 1 (RS): P1, *k1, p1; rep from *.
Rep Row 1 for pat.

SPECIAL ABBREVIATION
SBU = Slide 1 bead up to the RH needle into position indicated in pat.

Instructions

Pre-string approx 33 size 6/0 White Ceylon beads.

Cast on 135 sts.

Next Row (RS): Work Seed st over first 5 sts, pm, beg St st and knit to last 5 sts, pm, work Seed st to end of row.

Maintaining first and last 5 sts in Seed st throughout for side edge borders and St st in center, work even until piece measures approx 1½" from beg, ending with a WS row.

Beg with Row 1, work 7 reps (476 rows) of Tri-Bead pat between markers, then work Rows 1–3 once more. Shawl will measure approx 63".

Work St st between markers for approx 1½", ending with a WS row.

Bind off all sts loosely.

Finishing
Weave in loose yarn ends.

Stitch Beads to Shawl

See "Stitching Beads to Knitted Fabric," on page 78. Referring to the photo for placement of beads, bring needle up to RS of fabric and thread 1 each size 8/0 White Ceylon bead, size 8/0 Crystal bead, size 6/0 Lt. Sapphire bead, size 8/0 Crystal bead, and size 8/0 White Ceylon bead (5 beads). Take needle back to WS at a slight angle and securely fasten off. Rep over shawl.

Knotted Fringe

See the Glossary for general instructions for Knotted Fringe. For this project, cut 150 strands of yarn, each 36" long, for 50 fringes.

For each fringe, fold 3 strands in half, insert crochet hook from back to front through stitch at center point of cast-on edge, and pull the fold

through to back. Pull ends through the fold and secure. Evenly space 12 fringes along each side of center point to ends—25 fringes total.

Then, *beg at right edge, take one half of the strands from first fringe and knot them tog with half of the strands from the next fringe; cont in this manner to end.

Return to right edge, take rem half of the strands from first fringe and knot them tog with half of the strands from the next fringe; cont across to end. Rep from * once more.

Attach 25 fringes to bound-off edge and tie as above. Trim neatly to desired length.

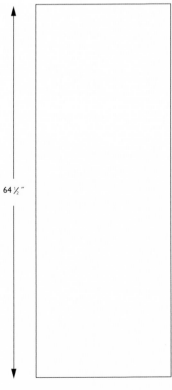

64½"

24½"

If you want a really "fun-knit" project, look no farther. This shrug is knit in the round, inside out, with beaded mock cables! For this design, I started with the stitch pattern. It's one of those patterns that just begs to be beaded. As you look through stitch pattern reference books for your own designs, try to visualize a bead embedded in a "valley" between stitches or in the hole made by a yarn-over in a lace pattern. Slip-stitch patterns are perfect to experiment with, using the slip-stitch technique for adding beads.

Although this pattern is worked in the round, the general instructions for Slip-Stitch Beaded Knitting (page 38) apply here as well. You will simply be working "around" rather than "across" to the desired bead position indicated in the pattern.

SKILL LEVEL Easy

SIZES XS (S, M, L). Instructions are for smallest size, with changes for other sizes noted in parentheses as necessary.

FINISHED MEASUREMENTS
Body (unstretched): approx 19 (21, 23¾, 25¼)"
Body (stretched to fit): approx 39 (43, 47½, 51½)"
Collar (unstretched): approx 22¼ (24¾, 27, 29½)"
Length: 12½ (12½, 12½, 13)"

MATERIALS
- Berroco *Cotton Twist* (70% mercerized cotton / 30% rayon, 85 yds/78m, 1.75 oz/50g): 6 (7, 8, 10) skeins # 8325 Navy Blue
- Approx 405 (445, 530, 625) size 6/0 Japanese Seed Beads (sample knit with #6-131 Crystal, from Caravan Beads)
- Size 8 (5mm) 24" circular knitting needle, or size needed to obtain gauge
- Stitch marker
- Bead-stringing needle
- Tapestry needle

GAUGE
In K2, P2 Rib, 31 sts and 25 rnds = 4"/10cm *unstretched.*
In Beaded Slipped Cable pat, 34 sts and 32 rnds = 4"/10cm *unstretched.*
To save time, take time to check gauge.

PATTERN STITCHES
K2, P2 RIB (MULT OF 4 STS)
Rnd 1: *P2, k2; rep from * to end of rnd.
Rep Rnd 1 for pat.

BEADED SLIPPED CABLE (MULT OF 5 STS)
Rnd 1: *P1, k1, SBU, k2, p1; rep from * around.
Rnds 2 and 3: *P1, sl 1 wyib, k2, p1; rep from * around.
Rnd 4: *P1, drop slipped st from needle to front of work, k2, pick up dropped st and knit it, p1; rep from * around.
Rep Rnds 1–4 for pat.

SPECIAL ABBREVIATION
SBU = Slide 1 bead up to the RH needle into position indicated in pat.

Instructions

Body
Cast on 148 (164, 180, 196) sts. Place marker and join, being careful not to twist sts.

Work in K2, P2 Rib pat until piece measures approx 12½ (12½, 12½, 13½)" from beg.

Work Purl Turning Ridge and Increase for Slipped Cable Pattern
Next Rnd: P13 (15, 17, 19), M1, *p3, M1; rep from * to last 12 (14, 16, 18) sts, purl to end—190 (210, 230, 250) sts. Cut yarn.

Collar
With a new skein of yarn, pre-string approx 170 beads.

Set Up Beaded Slipped Cable Pattern
Next Rnd: Join new skein, *p1, k3, p1; rep from * to end of rnd.

Beg with Rnd 2, work in Beaded

Pattern Notes
- *Shrug and collar are made in the round as a tube, then turned inside out so that when the collar is folded down at turning ridge, the RS is facing outward.*
- *This fabric is very stretchy. Refer to body (stretched to fit) measurement to determine correct size.*

Slipped Cable pat until collar measures approx 5½ (5½, 5½, 6½)" from beg, ending with Rnd 4. Bind off loosely in pat.

Finishing
Turn entire tube inside out, then fold collar down at turning ridge so that RS is facing the "public side."

Weave in loose yarn ends.

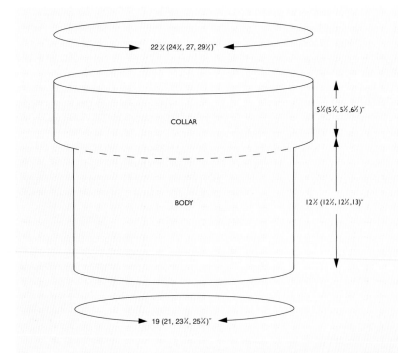

CHAPTER 5
Knitting with Beads Through a Stitch

$\mathcal{T}$his technique is most often confused with Bead Knitting. Think of those beautiful Victorian beaded bags that our great-grandmothers were so fond of. In true Bead Knitting, a bead is worked through every stitch of a motif or pattern so that you don't see any fabric, just beads. It's beautiful but very time-consuming, and is the most difficult of all the beading techniques.

Knitting with beads through a stitch would be referred to as Beaded Knitting where you add only enough beads to embellish your work. It's much easier and faster to work. Beads are pre-strung onto the working yarn as in the previous techniques, but the beads are actually slipped into a stitch, rather than between or in front of stitches. You can "knit" the bead through as you are knitting a stitch or "purl" the bead through as you are purling a stitch.

TECHNIQUE Knitting with Beads Through a Knit Stitch

1 *With pre-strung yarn, work across the row to the desired bead position indicated in the pattern or chart by BK1. Insert the knitting needle into the stitch to be knit as usual (above).*

2 *With the yarn at the back (WS) of the work, slide one bead up close to the needle, and knit both the yarn and the bead through the stitch (above). A little nudge with the left index finger helps to push the bead through the stitch.*

3 *To keep the bead stable, on the following row purl the stitch that the bead is on through the back loop, making sure that the bead is on the right side (RS) of the fabric (above). Tip: Insert the needle into the stitch above the bead to ensure that the bead falls to the front (RS) of the work.*

Sample fabric knit with beads either through a knit stitch or through a purl stitch.

In the charts for patterns using this technique (that is, where the bead is worked through a stitch), the bead is drawn within the square representing the stitch. You should work the bead along with the stitch as indicated in the chart (either knit or purled).

Occasionally you'll have a bead with a mind of its own that wants to slide down the "leg" of the stitch, through the center of the stitch below, landing on the strand between two stitches. If that happens, just gently guide it back into place. However, if it seems to be happening more than occasionally, it's probably because the bead is too small for the knitting or the stitches. Try using a bead that is a little larger (see the discussion of the different types of beads on page 10) or, if gauge is not critical, a smaller needle size so that the center of the stitch is a bit smaller.

TECHNIQUE Knitting with Beads Through a Purl Stitch

1 *With pre-strung yarn, work across the row to the desired bead position indicated in the pattern or chart by BP1. With the yarn in the front (RS) of the work in purl position, insert the knitting needle into the stitch to be purled as usual (above).*

2 *Slide one bead up close to the needle, and purl both the yarn and the bead through the stitch (above). A little nudge with the left thumb helps to push the bead through the stitch.*

3 *To keep the bead stable, on the following row knit the stitch that the bead is on through the back loop, making sure that the bead is on the right side (RS) of the fabric (above). Tip: Insert the needle into the stitch above the bead to ensure that the bead falls to the front (RS) of the work.*

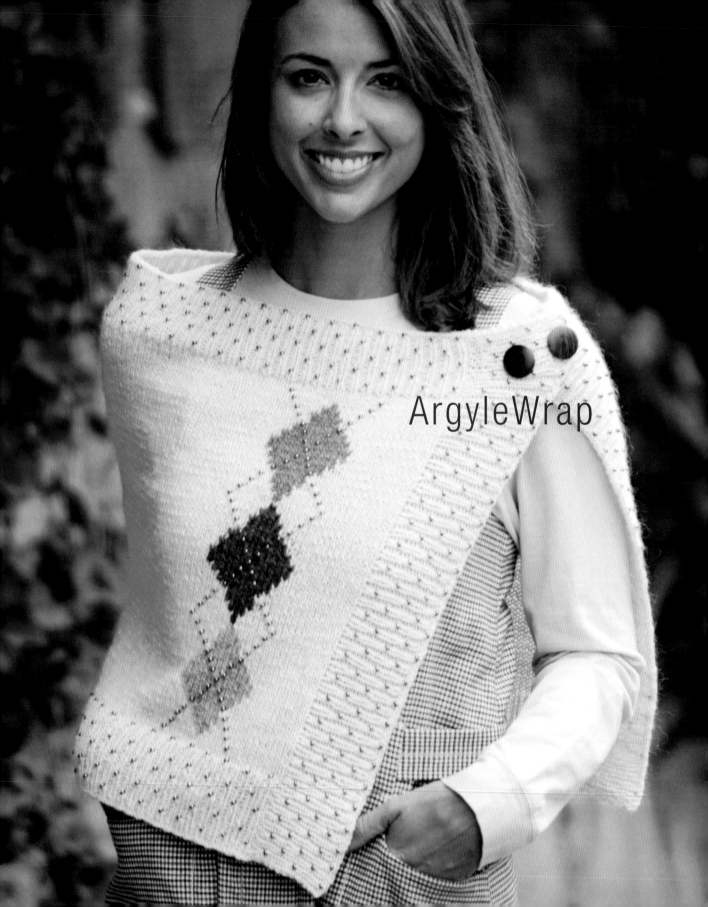

This preppy favorite is the perfect backdrop for, of course, beads! The argyle pattern takes center stage in pretty colors and X's knit-in with beads. The wrap is a simple rectangle, but it's framed in wide beaded ribbing to add a little *wow!* You'll use one knitting with beads technique worked in two different ways: knitting with beads through a knit stitch and knitting with beads through a purl stitch.

SKILL LEVEL Intermediate

SIZES S (M, L, XL). Instructions are for smallest size, with changes for other sizes noted in parentheses as necessary.

FINISHED MEASUREMENTS
Width: 37 (41½, 46, 50½)"
Length: 19½"

MATERIALS
- Green Mountain Spinnery *Mountain Mohair* (70% wool / 30% mohair, 140 yds/128m, 2 oz/57g): 5 (6, 7, 8) skeins Edelweiss (A); 1 skein each Pistachio (B), Clove (C), and Pink Pink (D)
- Approx 625 (675, 725, 775) size 6/0 Japanese Seed Beads (sample knit with #6-254D Transparent Dark Red AB, from Caravan Beads)
- One each size 7 (4.5mm) and 5 (3.75mm) 24" (29" for larger sizes) circular knitting needles, or sizes needed to obtain gauge
- Bead-stringing needle
- Tapestry needle
- Two 1⅛" (28mm) dark brown wooden buttons with shank

GAUGE
With larger needles in St st, 18 sts and 26 rows = 4"/10cm.
To save time, take time to check gauge.

PATTERN STITCHES
BEADED ARGYLE PATTERN (15-ST PANEL)
See Beaded Argyle chart.

BEADED K1, P1 RIB (MULT OF 4 STS + 2)
See Beaded K1, P1 Rib chart, or in words:
Row 1 (RS): *K1, p1; rep from * across.
Row 2: *K1, p1, k1, BP1; rep from * to last 2 sts, k1, p1.
Row 3: *K1, p1, k1-tbl, p1; rep from * to last 2 sts, k1, p1.
Rows 4 and 5: *K1, p1; rep from * across.
Row 6: K1, p1, k1, p1, *k1, BP1, k1, p1; rep from * to last 2 sts, k1, p1.
Row 7: K1, p1, *k1, p1, k1-tbl, p1; rep from * to last 4 sts, k1, p1, k1, p1.
Row 8: Work same as Row 4.
Rows 9–18: Rep Rows 1–8 once more, then rep Rows 1 and 2.

STOCKINETTE STITCH (ST ST)
Knit on RS rows, purl on WS rows.

SPECIAL ABBREVIATION
BP1 = Purl 1 bead through a purl st.

Instructions

With A, pre-string 173 (198, 223, 248) beads.

With larger needle, cast on 142 (162, 182, 202) sts.

Work Rows 1–18 of Beaded K1, P1 Rib pat from chart, or written-out instructions. Ribbing should measure approx 2¼" from beg.

Work 2 rows even in St st.

Cut yarn and pre-string approx 8 beads onto this partial skein of yarn. With a second skein of A, pre-string 22 beads. You now have 1 full skein of A for narrow side of body on the

Pattern Notes

- *A circular needle is used to accommodate the large number of sts. Work the Wrap back and forth in rows.*
- *When working the Beaded Argyle Patten, use intarsia technique (see Glossary) with separate lengths of yarn for each color. When switching from one color to the next, bring the new yarn up from under the previous yarn to lock sts and prevent holes.*

right side of diamond and 1 partial skein of A for long side of body on the left side of diamond.

BEADED ARGYLE

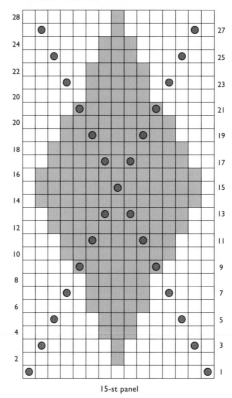

15-st panel

COLOR KEY
□ = A
▨ = B
▨ = C
▤ = D

STITCH KEY
□ = Knit on RS, purl on WS
● = Knit 1 bead

Pre-string 13 beads onto each of B, C, and D.

Next Row (RS): Re-attach the partial skein of A. K11, pm, work Row 1 of Beaded Argyle pat from chart over next 15 sts, pm, knit to end of row.

On following row, cont in pat as est, joining B as indicated in chart, then join full skein of A, and work to end of row.

Cont in St st, working Beaded Argyle pat between markers until chart has been completed.

Work 28-row Beaded Argyle chart twice more, first working diamond in C, then working diamond in D.

With A, work Row 1 of chart once more, then work 3 rows St st.

Cut yarn, and pre-string 175 (200, 225, 250) beads.

Re-attach yarn, change to smaller needles, and work Rows 1–18 in Beaded K1, P1 Rib pat.

Bind off loosely in pat.

Finishing

With A, pre-string 128 beads.

Button Band (Left Front)

With RS facing and smaller needles, pick up and knit 106 sts evenly along left front edge. Work Rows 1–18 of Beaded K1, P1 Rib pat. Bind off. Place markers for 2 buttons evenly spaced 1½" from top edge.

Buttonhole Band (Right Front)

Work same as for Left Front until band measures approx 1", ending with a RS row.

Buttonhole Row (WS): Rib 8, bind off 2 sts, work to end of row.

Next Row: Work in rib as est, and cast on 2 sts over bound-off sts.

Cont in rib as est until the band measures approx 2½", then rep Buttonhole Row. Complete same as for Left Front.

Weave in loose yarn ends.

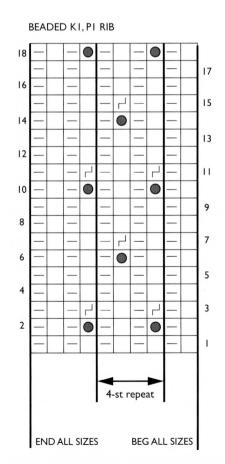

BEADED K1, P1 RIB

4-st repeat

END ALL SIZES   BEG ALL SIZES

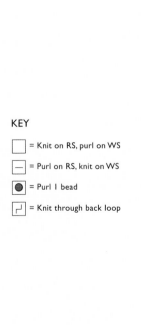

KEY

☐ = Knit on RS, purl on WS

— = Purl on RS, knit on WS

⬤ = Purl 1 bead

⌐| = Knit through back loop

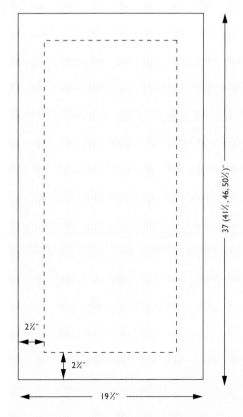

2¾"

2¼"

19½"

37 (41½, 46, 50½)"

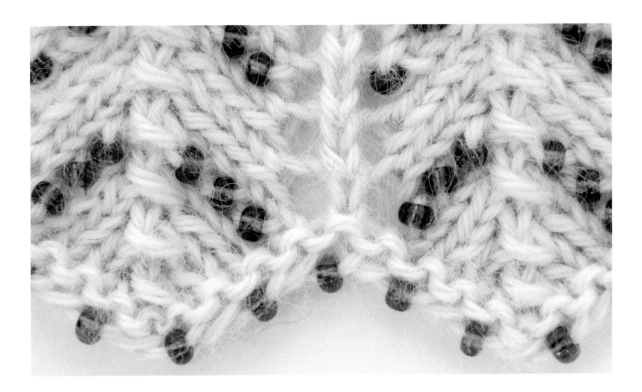

Lace patterns lend themselves to beads beautifully. Beads add emphasis to scalloped edges and follow the lines of slanting stitches created by increases and decreases. This lace pattern, although lovely by itself, becomes simply elegant with the addition of these sapphire beads.

SKILL LEVEL Intermediate

SIZES S (M/L). Instructions are for smallest size, with changes for other sizes noted in parentheses as necessary.

FINISHED MEASUREMENTS
Width at lower edge: 47½ (52)"
Shoulder width: 37½ (43)"
Length: 16¾ (18¾)"

MATERIALS
- Plymouth *Baby Alpaca* D.K. (100% baby alpaca, 125 yds/114m, 1.75oz/50g): 7 (9) skeins #100
- Approx 1575 (1715) size 6/0 Czech Seed Beads (sample knit with #667 Sapphire, from The Bead Wrangler)
- Size 5 (3.75mm) 24" and 29" circular needles, or size needed to obtain gauge
- Size 6 (4.25mm) 24" and 29" circular needles, or size needed to obtain gauge
- Size 7 (4.5mm) knitting needle for 3-needle bind-off
- 1½ yds 2" blue satin ribbon to match beads
- Bead-stringing needle
- Tapestry needle

GAUGE
With smaller needles in Beaded Lace Pat, 28 sts and 30 rows = 4"/10cm.
With larger needles in St st, 22 sts and 28 rows = 4"/10cm.
To save time, take time to check gauge.

PATTERN STITCHES
BEADED LACE PATTERN (MULT OF 10 STS + 3)
See chart, or in words:
Row 1 (RS): K2, *yo, BK1, k2, sk2p, k2, BK1, yo, k1; rep from * to last st, k1.
Row 2: P1, *p2, p1-tbl, p5, p1-tbl, p1; rep from * to last 2 sts, p2.
Row 3: K2, *yo, k1, BK1, k1, sk2p, k1, BK1, k1, yo, k1; rep from * to last st, k1.
Row 4: P1, *p3, p1-tbl, p3, p1-tbl, p2; rep from * to last 2 sts, p2.
Row 5: K2, *yo, k2, BK1, sk2p, BK1, k2, yo, k1; rep from * to last st, k1.
Row 6: P1, *p4, p1-tbl, p1, p1-tbl, p3; rep from * to last 2 sts, p2.
Rep Rows 1–6 for pat.

GARTER STITCH
Knit every row.

STOCKINETTE STITCH (ST ST)
Knit on RS rows, purl on WS rows.

K1, P1 RIB (MULT OF 2 STS +1)
Row 1 (RS): *K1, p1; rep from * to last st, k1.
Row 2: *P1, k1; rep from * to last st, p1.
Rep Rows 1–2 for pat.

SPECIAL ABBREVIATION
BK1 = Knit 1 bead through a st.

Instructions

Beaded Cast-on Edge
See "Casting on Stitches with Beads," on page 13. Pre-string 165 (180) beads. Unwind enough yarn from skein to cast on 333 (363) sts using the long-tail cast-on technique (see Glossary).

Slide beads down strand so that they are on the "tail" coming from the skein. With smaller needles, make a slip knot and place on needle, then cast on 1 more st (2 sts on needle).

*Slip 1 bead up close to needle, then cast on 2 sts. Rep from * until you have 332 (362) sts on needle, then cast on 1 last st—333 (363) sts.

Work 3 rows even in Garter st.

Cut yarn, and pre-string approx 462 beads. Rejoin yarn.

Beg with Row 1, work 6 reps of Beaded Lace pat. Piece will measure approx 4¼" from beg.

Next Row (RS): K2, k2tog, k1, sk2p, k1, ssk; [k4, sk2p, k3] 15 (16) times; k1, k2tog, k1, sk2p, k1, ssk; [k4, sk2p, k3] 15 (17) times; end row k1, k2tog, k1, sk2p, k1, ssk, k2—261 (285) sts.

Change to larger needles, and work 5 (7) rows in St st, beg with WS row.

Dec Row (RS): K63 (69), [sk2p, k63 (69)] 3 times—255 (279) sts.

Work 3 (5) rows even in St st.

Dec Row (RS): K62 (68), sk2p, [k61 (67) sts, sk2p] 2 times, k62 (68)—249 (273) sts.

Cont to dec in this manner, working 1 fewer st before first dec and after last dec, and 2 fewer sts between decs each Dec Row, every 4th (6th) row 7 (6) times—207 (237) sts.

Cont even until piece measures approx 10½ (12)" from beg, ending with a WS row.

Shape Shoulders and Neck
Cont working decs as est on next row, then every other row 13 (15) times—123 (141) sts.

Purl one row.

Next Row (RS): K9 (12), k2tog, [k6 (3), k2tog] 13 (23) times, k8 (12)—109 (117) sts.

Neckband
Next Row (WS): Change to smaller needles. *P1, k1; rep from * across row to last st, p1. Cont in K1, P1 Rib pat as est until band measures approx 2" from beg, ending with a WS row.

Next Row (RS): Rib 9 (14), k2tog, [rib 16 (27), k2tog] 5 (3) times, rib 8 (14)—103 (113) sts. Leave sts on needle.

Beaded Lace Collar
Pre-string 171 (188) beads—51 (56) beads for Beaded Cast-on Edge, 120 (132) beads for Beaded Lace pat.

With smaller needles, working Beaded Cast-on Edge same as for Capelet, cast on 103 (113) sts.

Work 3 rows even in Garter st.

Work 2 reps of Beaded Lace pat, beg with Row 1. Piece will measure approx 2" from beg. Leave sts on needle.

Attach Collar with 3-Needle Bind-off

See the Glossary for general guidance for 3-Needle Bind-off. For this project, place the needle holding sts for the collar in front of the needle holding sts for neckband so that the WS of the collar is facing the RS of the neckband. The needle points of both needles should be pointing toward the right.

With size 7 needle, *knit first st from the front needle (collar) together with the first st from the back needle (neckband)—1 st on needle.

Knit next st from each needle in same manner, then bind off 1 st; rep from * until all sts have been knit together and bound off. Fasten off last st. Tack collar down around neckband as needed.

Front Bands

With RS facing and smaller needles, pick up and knit 92 (104) sts along left front edge of Capelet (do not pick up through collar sts). Work 3 rows in Garter st. Bind off. Rep for right front edge.

Thread ribbon around neck between collar and neckband. Trim edges as desired. Weave in loose yarn ends.

BEADED LACE

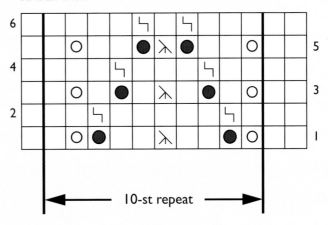

10-st repeat

KEY

⬤ = Knit 1 bead

☐ = Knit on RS, purl on WS

⅂ = Purl through the back loop

○ = Yarn over

⅄ = Slip 1 stitch, k2tog, pass the slipped stitch over

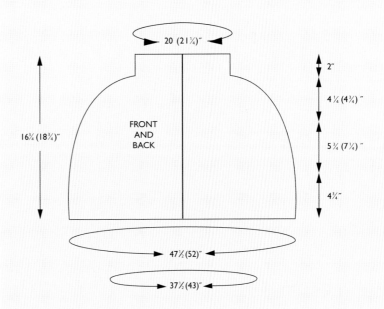

20 (21¼)"

2"

4¼ (4¾)"

5¾ (7¼)"

4¾"

16¾ (18¾)"

FRONT AND BACK

47½ (52)"

37½ (43)"

CHAPTER 6
Knitting with Beads on a Yarn-over

*Y*arn-over (yo) stitches found in lace patterns, such as the pretty mesh Vertical Lace Trellis Pattern on page 66, are ideal for adding beads to knitting. It's a little trickier than with the other techniques to keep the bead in place as you are working the stitch, but you can easily master it with just a little practice.

TECHNIQUE

1 *Work across the row to the desired bead position indicated in the pattern or chart by Byo. Bring the yarn forward to the right side (RS) of your work between the two needles. Slide one bead up close to the right-hand needle (above).*

2 *Then work the yarn-over (yo) in the normal way, holding the bead in place with your thumb (above).*

3 *On the following row, work the yo, making sure that the bead remains on the right side (RS). You can use your thumb to give it just a little nudge toward the front (above).*

Sample fabric knit with beads on a yarn-over.

SpringMornShawl

Mesh or open-work stitch patterns have certainly seen a return to popularity. And no wonder. They are easy to knit, work up beautifully on almost any size needle, and are perfect for a rectangle shawl. The use of a yarn-over to create the "holes" in these patterns is typical. So that's where we'll add a bead. As mentioned in chapter 1, the bone beads and organic cotton in this yarn make a perfect combination . . . and a beautiful shawl for a chilly spring morning walk.

SKILL LEVEL Easy

SIZE One size

APPROXIMATE FINISHED MEASUREMENTS
Width: 11¼"
Length: 30½"

MATERIALS
- Green Mountain Spinnery *Cotton Comfort* (20% organic cotton / 80% fine wool, 180 yds/165m, 2 oz/57g): 3 skeins #62201 Peony
- Approx 175 3 x 4mm Bone Beads, Natural
- Size 8 (5mm) knitting needles, or size needed to obtain gauge
- Bead-stringing needle
- Crochet hook for fringe
- Tapestry needle

GAUGE
In Beaded Vertical Lace Trellis pat st, 16 sts and 28 rows = 4"/10cm.
To save time, take time to check gauge.

PATTERN STITCH
BEADED VERTICAL LACE TRELLIS PATTERN (MULT OF 8 STS + 5)
Row 1 and all WS rows: Sl 1, purl to last st, k1.
Rows 2, 6, 10, 14 (RS): Sl 1, k1, *yo, k2tog; rep from * to last st, k1.
Row 4 (RS): Sl 1, *ssk, Byo, [ssk, yo] 3 times; rep from * across row to last 4 sts, ssk, Byo, k2.
Rows 8 and 16 (RS): Sl 1, *ssk, yo; rep from * across row to last 2 sts, k2.
Row 12 (RS): Sl 1, [ssk, yo] 2 times, ssk, Byo, *[ssk, yo] 3 times, ssk, Byo; rep from * to last 6 sts, [ssk, yo] 2 times, k2.
Rep Rows 1–16 for pat.

SPECIAL ABBREVIATION
BYO = Slide 1 bead up to the RH needle, then work a yo in the usual way, holding the bead in place on the RS with your thumb.

Instructions

Pre-string approx 105 beads.

Using knit-on cast-on technique (see Glossary), loosely cast on 45 sts.

Beg with Row 1, work Beaded Lace pat until piece measures approx 30½", ending with Row 6.

Bind off very loosely. (Using a needle one size larger to bind off will help keep your bind-off edge loose.)

Finishing
Weave in loose yarn ends.

Fringe
See the Glossary for general instructions for Simple Fringe. For this

project, cut 288 strands of yarn, each 12" long, for 48 fringes. For each fringe, fold 6 strands in half, insert crochet hook from back to front through stitch, and pull fold through to back. Pull ends through fold and pull tightly.

Evenly fringe along cast-on, bound-off, and bottom edges. Trim fringes neatly to desired length.

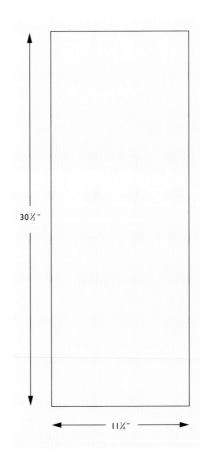

30½"

11¼"

CHAPTER 7
Hook Beading

$\mathcal{S}$ometimes pre-stringing beads is neither necessary nor practical. For instance, you may want to add just a sprinkling of beads to your knitting and question the need to pre-string just a few beads, constantly pushing them down the strand and out of your way. Or if you are using a delicate yarn, such as the alpaca/Tencel blend used for the Bobbles and Beads Capelet on page 74, the friction caused by sliding the beads may weaken or damage the yarn. Or perhaps a bead has a definite shape, such as a tulip or a heart, but the hole runs through its center from top to bottom. Of course, you would like the bead to sit upright on your knitting.

No problem. There is a way to knit in beads without pre-stringing. It's Hook Beading, which is done with a small steel crochet hook. In the charts for patterns using this technique (that is, where the bead is hooked onto the stitch), the bead is drawn within the square representing the stitch. You should work the stitch as indicated in the chart after hooking the bead.

TECHNIQUE

1 *Work across the row to the desired bead position indicated in the pattern or chart by HB1. First, with a crochet hook, hook the bead (above).*

2 *Then hook the next stitch from the left-hand needle (above).*

3 *Pull the stitch through the bead (above), return it to the left-hand needle, then either slip the stitch purlwise to the right-hand needle, or knit it as instructed in the pattern.*

Sample fabric knit with Hook Beading.

What a pretty place for a bead—a bow! Here's another one of those stitch patterns that you can easily adapt to knitting with beads. Hook Beading works perfectly here. And, of course, the big advantage is that there's no need to pre-string.

The stitch pattern alone creates a beautiful textured fabric for this colorful ponchini.

SKILL LEVEL Easy

SIZES S/M (L/XL). Instructions are for smallest size, with changes for other sizes noted in parentheses as necessary.

FINISHED MEASUREMENTS
Width: 13½ (15)"
Length: 46 (52½)"

MATERIALS
- Classic Elite Yarns *Provence* (100% mercerized cotton, 205 yds/186m, 3.5 oz/100g): 4 (5) hanks #2651 Pure Peri (A)
- Classic Elite Yarns *Bangles* (38% viscose / 36% Tactel nylon / 26% nylon, 83 yds/76mm, 1.75 oz/50g): 2 balls #6704 Heliotrope (B)
- Approx 300 (375) size 6/0 Pony Beads (sample knit with #16615 Frosted Citrus, from Wichelt Imports/Mill Hill)
- Size 6 (4.25mm) knitting needles, or size needed to obtain gauge
- Size 9 (1.25mm) steel crochet hook
- Tapestry needle

GAUGE
In Beaded Bows pat, 22 sts and 36 rows = 4"/10cm.
To save time, take time to check gauge.

PATTERN STITCHES
BEADED BOWS PATTERN (MULT OF 9 STS + 11)
Rows 1 and 3 (RS): Knit.
Rows 2 and 4: Purl.
Rows 5, 7, and 9: K4, sl 3 sts wyif, *k6, sl 3 sts wyif; rep from * to last 4 sts, k4.
Rows 6 and 8: Purl.
Row 10: P5, *on next st (which is center st of 3 slipped sts) insert LH needle down through the 3 loose strands and purl the 3 strands tog with the next st on needle as one, p8; rep from *, ending last rep p5.
Row 11: K5, HB1, *k8, HB1; rep from * to last 5 sts, k5.
Row 12: Purl.
Rep Rows 1–12 for pat.

GARTER STITCH
Knit every row.

SPECIAL ABBREVIATION
HB1 = Hook 1 bead.

Instructions

With A, cast on 74 (83) sts.

Work even in Beaded Bows pat until piece measures approx 46 (52½)" from beg, ending with Row 4 of pat.

Bind off.

Finishing
Side Borders
With RS facing and B, pick up and knit 209 (236) sts evenly along one side edge of rectangle. Knit 1 row.

Pattern Note

This ponchini is worked as a rectangle, then joined with a seam along one short and one long edge (see diagram).

Inc Row (RS): K1, M1, knit to last st, M1, k1.

Cont in Garter st, work Inc Row every other row until border measures approx 1", ending with a WS row. Bind off loosely. Rep for other side edge.

Top and Bottom Borders

With RS facing and B, pick up and knit 74 (82) sts evenly across cast-on edge. Work same as for Side Borders. Bind off. Rep for bound-off edge.

Sew mitered corners tog.

Sew one short end to one long edge of rectangle (see diagram).

Weave in loose yarn ends.

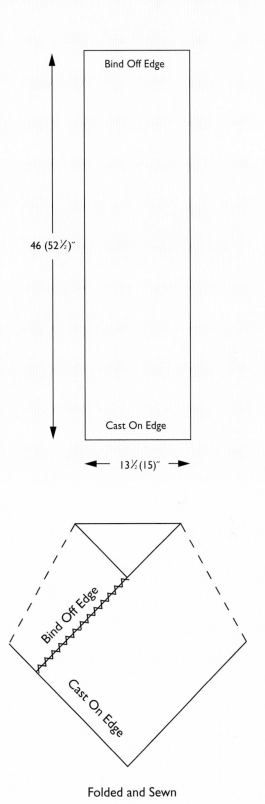

Bind Off Edge

46 (52½)″

Cast On Edge

13½ (15)″

Bind Off Edge

Cast On Edge

Folded and Sewn

BobblesandBeadsCapelet

This yarn is so beautiful . . . but it's delicate. Using the Hook Beading technique (page 68) to add beads is the best way to avoid damage to the fragile fibers. You may actually prefer Hook Beading to the other techniques since no pre-stringing is necessary. As long as there are not too many beads to hook, you will find hooking on beads to be a minimal interruption as you knit, not unlike using a cable needle when knitting cables.

SKILL LEVEL Intermediate

SIZES XS (S, M, L, XL). Instructions are for smallest size, with changes for other sizes noted in parentheses as necessary.

FINISHED MEASUREMENTS
Circumference: 41½ (46, 50½, 55¼, 59¾)"
Length: 12½ (12½, 12½, 14, 14)"

MATERIALS
- Classic Elite Yarns *Miracle* (50% alpaca / 50% Tencel, 108 yds/99m, 1.75 oz/50g): 5 (6, 7, 8, 8) skeins # 3304 Palm Beach Blue
- Approx 225 (250, 275, 290, 310) size 6/0 Japanese Seed Beads (sample knit with #6-275 Dark Peach Lined Crystal AB, from Caravan Beads)
- Size 4 (3.5mm) 29" circular needle
- Size 6 (4.25mm) 29" circular needle, or size needed to obtain gauge
- Size 9 (1.25mm) steel crochet hook
- 1¾ yds" [3/8" wide] satin ribbon for drawstring
- Tapestry needle

GAUGE
With larger needle in Beaded Brocade pat, 21 sts and 28 rows = 4"/10cm.
To save time, take time to check gauge.

PATTERN STITCHES
BEADED BROCADE PATTERN (MULT OF 12 STS + 14)
See chart.

GARTER STITCH
Knit every row.

SPECIAL ABBREVIATION
HB1 = Hook 1 bead.

Instructions

With smaller needles, cast on 218 (242, 266, 290, 314) sts.

Work in Garter st for approx 1", ending with a WS row.

Change to larger needles, and work Rows 1–14 of Beaded Brocade pat, then rep Rows 3–14 four (4, 4, 5, 5) times more, finishing with Rows 15–23. Piece will measure approx 11½ (11½, 11½, 13, 13)" from beg.

Change to smaller needles, and work in Garter st for approx ½", ending with a WS row.

Drawstring Eyelet Row (RS): K3, *yo twice, k2tog, k4; rep from * to last 5 sts, end yo twice, k2tog, k3.

Next Row: Knit across, working first yo and dropping second yo from needle.

Cont in Garter st until band measures approx 1", ending with a WS row. Bind off loosely.

Finishing
Fold rectangle in half widthwise,

with WS sides tog. Beg at top (neck edge), sew side seam, leaving bottom 4" (or desired length for slit) open for side slit.

Slit Edging
With RS facing and smaller needles, beg at cast-on edge, pick up and knit 18 sts evenly along one side of slit. Knit 1 row, then bind off. Rep for other side, beg at seam edge.

Weave in loose yarn ends.

Weave ribbon through Drawstring Eyelet Row; gather to desired fit, and tie in bow.

BEADED BROCADE

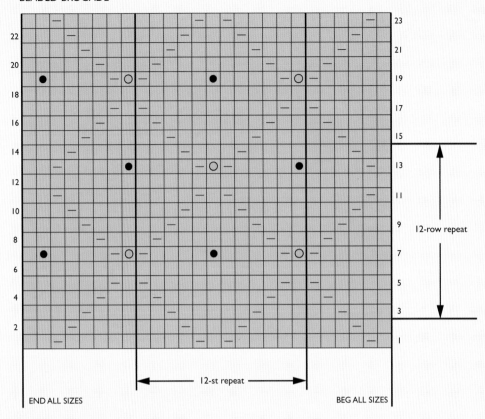

12-row repeat

12-st repeat

END ALL SIZES

BEG ALL SIZES

KEY

⬜ = Knit on RS, purl on WS

— = Purl on RS, knit on WS

● = Bobble: Knit into front, back, front, back and front of next st (5 sts made from 1 st), turn; p5, turn; k2tog-tbl, k3tog, pass k2tog over k3tog

○ = Hook Bead: First hook a bead, then hook the next stitch from the left needle. Pull the stitch through the bead, return it to the left needle and knit

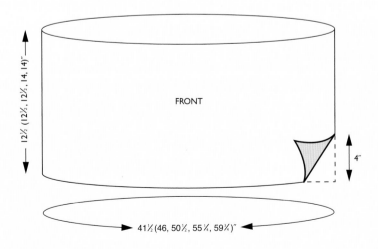

FRONT

12½ (12½, 12½, 14, 14)"

4"

41½ (46, 50½, 55¼, 59¾)"

CHAPTER 8
Stitching Beads to Knitted Fabric

You may want to add just a touch of beads to your project (say, a little flower or a geometric design) . . . or perhaps you have found the most beautiful beads in your favorite bead store but they are way too tiny to knit with . . . or maybe you'd just like to fill in some areas that have already been beaded. Whatever your motivation, you might want to try stitching beads to your finished knitting projects. It's a great choice if you are a fan of novelty yarns, most of which are too thick or bumpy or furry to strand with beads. Think of it as embroidery . . . with beads.

There are beading needles and beading threads specifically made for beading purposes. You can use one of the specialty needles or a sharp sewing needle that has a small enough eye for the hole of the bead to pass over. Beading threads come in a wide range of colors and can be made of nylon, silk, twisted polyester, or mercerized cotton. The thread you choose will depend on the bead and the fabric. Make sure you choose a sturdy yarn that will support the weight of the beads.

When stitching beads to knitted fabric, work in small motifs or in a staggered pattern. Stitching too many beads in a straight line in one area will restrict the fabric's ability to stretch.

TECHNIQUE

1 Use a beading needle with an eye small enough to fit through the hole of the bead, and use beading thread that matches the yarn and the bead. Bring the needle up through a stitch, piercing the fibers of the yarn, rather than through the center hole of the stitch (above).

2 Thread the bead(s) onto the needle and thread.

3 Take the needle back down into the fabric, again piercing the fibers of the yarn.

Sample fabric with beads stitched to the fabric.

Houndstooth Stole

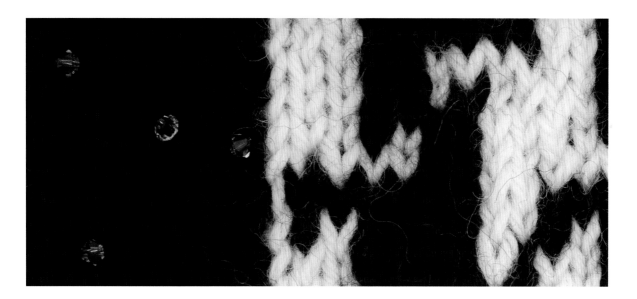

Bicone crystal beads, which have teeny-tiny holes, are just about impossible to knit with. But I love them! So when I decided to design a stole that I could wear with anything from jeans to a cocktail dress (okay, I really don't wear cocktail dresses, but just in case I do, I'll have something to wear with them), I went for black and white with a classic houndstooth pattern combined with color block, trimmed with black bicone crystals. Stunning! The crystals are quite easy to stitch in place, it's not terribly time-consuming to do, and no pattern is required for placement. Use as many or as few as you would like.

SIZE One size

FINISHED MEASUREMENTS
Width: 17½"
Length: 64"

MATERIALS
- Lion Brand Yarn *Lion Wool* (100% wool, 158 yds/144m, 3 oz/85 gms): 5 skeins #153 Ebony (A) and 3 skeins #099 Winter White (B)
- Approx 500 4mm Diamond Bicone Black Crystals
- Size 6 (4.25mm) 29" circular needle
- Size 8 (5mm) knitting needles, or size needed to obtain gauge
- Black beading thread
- Beading needle
- Tapestry needle

GAUGE
With larger needles in Houndstooth Check, 20 sts and 21 rows = 4"/10cm.
With larger needles in Double Moss st, 18 sts and 26 rows = 4"/10cm.
To save time, take time to check gauge.

PATTERN STITCHES
HOUNDSTOOTH CHECK (MULT OF 8 STS + 2)
See chart.

DOUBLE MOSS ST (MULT OF 4 STS + 2)
Row 1 (RS): K1 (selv st), *k2, p2; rep from * to last st, k1 (selv st).
Row 2: P1, *k2, p2; rep from * to last st, p1.
Row 3: K1, *p2, k2; rep from * to last st, k1.
Row 4: P1, *p2, k2; rep from * to last st, p1.
Rep Rows 1–4 for pat.

GARTER STITCH
Knit every row.

Instructions

With larger needles and A, cast on 74 sts. Join B, and beg with Row 1, work Houndstooth Check pat from chart until piece measures approx 8½", ending with Row 12 of chart.

Next Row (RS): K5, k2tog, [k7, k2tog] 7 times, k4—66 sts.

Next Row: Change to B and purl across.

With B, and beg with Row 1, work in Double Moss st pat for approx 10", ending with Row 3.

Next Row (WS): Change to A and purl across.

With A, and beg with Row 1, work Double Moss st for approx 14½", ending with Row 4.

Next Row (RS): K5, M1, [k8, M1] 7 times, k5—74 sts.

Next Row: Purl across.

Join A, and beg with Row 1, work Houndstooth Check pat for approx 18", ending with Row 12.

Next Row (RS): With A, k5, k2tog, [k7 sts, k2tog] 7 times, k4—66 sts.

Next Row: Change to B and purl across.

With B, and beg with Row 1, work Double Moss st for approx 10½", ending with Row 4.

Bind off all sts loosely.

Finishing

Side Borders
With RS facing and A, pick up and knit 283 sts along one long side edge of stole. Knit 1 row.

Inc Row (RS): K1, M1, knit to last st, M1, k1.

Cont in Garter st, work Inc Row every other row until border measures approx 1½", ending with a WS row. Bind off loosely. Rep for other side edge.

Top and Bottom Borders

With RS facing and A, pick up and knit 58 sts evenly across cast-on edge. Work same as for Side Borders. Bind off loosely. Rep for bound-off edge.

Sew mitered corners tog. Weave in loose yarn ends.

Stitch beads to side, top, and bottom borders in a staggered pattern as desired.

HOUNDSTOOTH CHECK

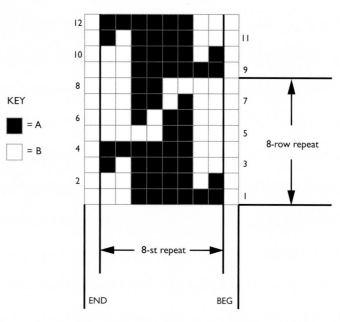

KEY

■ = A

□ = B

CHAPTER 9
Knitting with Sequins

*O*h-la-la! Shiny, shimmering, sexy sequins! Yes, you can even knit with sequins. Sequins are a little more challenging to work with than beads. The holes are smaller, the sequins are almost paper thin, and usually larger than beads, which makes them a bit more difficult to slip through a stitch. As with beads, you need to pre-string sequins onto the yarn before beginning to knit. Given the tiny holes in most sequins, you are limited in terms of the weight of yarn you can use. You might need to work using a second strand of very lightweight yarn (or thread) that you've pre-strung with the sequins; knit it in as you would when knitting with two strands held together.

You must string the sequins properly to ensure that they lie correctly on the fabric; not doing so can alter the finished look of the piece. If the sequin is cupped, you should string the cupped side (which is faceted and reflects the most light) toward the skein so that it faces outward once it is knitted into the fabric.

This book uses one of several different techniques for knitting with sequins—in this case, we're using ring-type sequins. Other methods may be used with different styles of sequins. Determining the method to use will depend mostly upon the sequin and how you want your finished project to look.

TECHNIQUE

1 *The ring-type sequins used for the Shimmering Shawlette (page 86) are great to work with. The hole is larger than in a traditional sequin, so you are not as limited in terms of the weight of yarn you can use and you can see the hole much more easily. String these sequins so that the embossed (bumpy) side is facing away from the ball of yarn and the cupped side is facing the ball of yarn (above).*

2 *Sequins are a little more difficult to separate than beads. Slide a small group of sequins up at one time. Press the group flat against the strand of yarn with your thumb and forefinger, then use your thumbnail to separate one sequin from the group (above). With pre-strung yarn, work across the row to the stitch where the sequin is to be added. Bring the yarn forward between the needles to the right side (RS), slide one sequin up close to the work, then purl the next stitch.*

ShimmeringShawlette

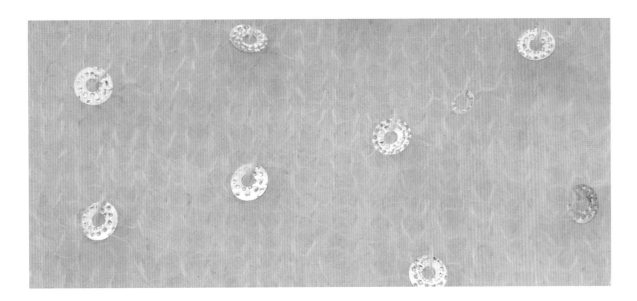

A favorite among lace knitters, this kid mohair and silk-blend yarn creates a "halo" to wrap around your shoulders, and sequins add a delicious shimmer. This little shawl is perfect for a stroll along a river walk or an evening out in your most elegant gown.

SIZES S (L). Instructions are for smallest size, with changes for other sizes noted in parentheses as necessary.

FINISHED MEASUREMENTS
Width at neck edge: Approx 28¼ (34½)"
Width at bottom edge: Approx 40½ (46¼)"
Length: 10 (12½)"

MATERIALS
- Rowan *Kidsilk Haze* (70% super kid mohair / 30% silk, 229 yds/210m, .90 oz/25g): 3 (4) skeins #590 Pearl
- One 1750ct package size 4mm Ring Sequins, and one 750ct package size 6mm Ring Sequins (sample knit with #MTC71-AM1, 4mm Silver Embossed Metallic Ring, and #MTC81-AM1, 6mm Silver Embossed Metallic Ring, from Cartwright's Sequins)
- Size 7 (4.5mm) knitting needles, or size needed to obtain gauge
- Bead-stringing needle
- Two stitch markers
- Tapestry needle

GAUGE
In St st, 22 sts and 32 rows = 4"/10cm.
To save time, take time to check gauge.

PATTERN STITCHES
STOCKINETTE STITCH (ST ST)
Knit on RS rows, purl on WS rows.

SEED STITCH (EVEN NUMBER OF STS)
Row 1 (RS): *K1, p1; rep from * across row.
Row 2: *P1, k1; rep from * across row.
Rep Rows 1 and 2 for pat.

SEQUIN PATTERN
Use the illustration as a guide for placing sequins to re-create the look of our model garment. or design your own. One knitter suggested making a template on a 4" x 4" card, drawing in the sequins where you would like them placed, then repeating that template as you would when using a typical chart.

Instructions

Pre-string approx 100 sequins, randomly alternating between 4mm and 6mm sequins as desired for placement.

Body

Beg at neck edge, cast on 158 (190) sts.

Work in Seed st for approx 1", beg and end with Row 1.

Beg with a WS row, work in St st and beg placing sequins **AND AT SAME TIME** inc 1 st (M1) at beg and end of every other row 32 (22) times, then every 4th row 0 (10) times—222 (254) sts. Work even if necessary until piece measures approx 9 (11½)" from beg, ending with a WS row.

Work in Seed st for approx 1", ending with a WS row.

Bind off loosely in pat.

Right Tie

With RS facing, pick up and knit 42 (50) sts (approx 1 st in every other row) along right-hand side (short edge) of shawlette.

Next Row (WS): Work in Seed st across first 6 sts, pm, purl to last 6 sts, pm, work in Seed st to end row.

Maintaining first and last 6 sts in Seed st for borders, work in St st

between markers and place sequins as for shawlette. *We used only size 4mm sequins for the ties on our sample.* Work even until tie measures approx 16" from beg, ending with a WS row.

Dec Row 1 (RS): Work in pat as est to 2 sts before second marker, k2tog, slip marker, work to end of row— 41 (49) sts.

Dec Row 2: Work to first marker, slip marker, p2tog, work in pat as est to end of row— 40 (48) sts.

Rep last 2 rows until 18 sts rem.

Next Row (RS): K2tog across row—9 sts.

Next Row: K2tog across row, ending row k1—5 sts.

Next Row: K2tog twice, k1—3 sts.

Bind off.

Left Tie
Work as for Right Tie to Dec Row 1.

Dec Row 1 (RS): Work to first marker, slip marker, ssk, work to end of row—41 (49) sts.

Dec Row 2: Work in pat as est to 2 sts before second marker, ssp, slip marker, work to end of row— 40 (48) sts.

Cont as for Right Tie.

Finishing
Weave in loose yarn ends.

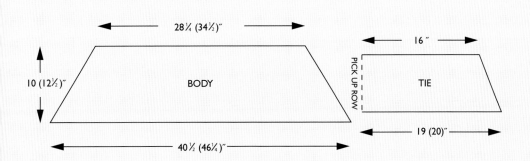

BODY 28¼ (34½)" 10 (12½)" 40½ (46¼)"

TIE PICK UP ROW 16" 19 (20)"

Glossary of Terms and Techniques

Bind-offs

Picot Bind-off
See instructions for Sassy Shrug, on page 26.

3-Needle Bind-off
Use this technique to join two pieces together by binding them off at the same time.

With the needle points of both needles pointing to the right, *knit the first stitch from the front needle together with the first stitch from the back needle—1 stitch on left-hand needle (see two photos above). Knit the next stitch from each needle in the same manner, then bind off 1 stitch; repeat from * until all stitches have been knit together, then bound off. Fasten off the last stitch.

Cables

Cables are made simply by taking a group of stitches and placing them on a cable needle, holding the cable needle either to the back or to the front of your work, working the next group of stitches, then working the first group of stitches from the cable needle.

If you hold the cable needle to the back of your work, the cable will twist to the right.

If the cable needle is held to the front of your work, the cable will twist to the left.

Cast-ons

Picot Cast-on
See instructions for Sassy Shrug, on page 26.

Long-tail Cast-on (or slingshot technique)
Unwind approximately 1" of yarn per stitch to be cast on (tail).

1 *Make a slip knot and place it on the right-hand needle for your first stitch.*

2 *Wrap the tail end around your left thumb and the yarn coming from the ball around your left index finger. Secure the strands in the palm of your hand with your other three fingers (will resemble holding a slingshot). Insert the right-hand needle from the outside into the loop on your thumb.*

3 *Catch the strand around the inside of your index finger, and pull it through the loop between your thumb and needle.*

4 *Drop the loop off your thumb and tighten onto the needle (1 new stitch). Continue in this manner until the desired number of stitches have been cast on.*

Knit-on Cast-on
It's not necessary to unwind yarn for each stitch. Just unwind enough to allow for weaving in the yarn end.

1 *Make a slip knot and place it on the left-hand needle for your first stitch.*

2 **Knit the stitch, drawing the yarn through to form a loop, but do not drop the stitch from the needle.*

3 *Place the loop (new stitch) onto the left-hand needle as shown. Rep from * for desired number of stitches.*

Charts

Read charts from bottom to top. Right-side rows are worked from right to left, and wrong-side rows are worked from left to right; the row numbers are written at the sides of the chart (right-side rows at right, wrong-side rows at left). When working in the round, always read the chart from right to left, because you are always working on right-side rows. Begin and end the chart where indicated, working the pattern repeat as many times as necessary for the number of stitches on your needles, then work the stitches following the repeat (if there are any) to end the row. Each square on a chart's graph represents 1 stitch. The symbol or color within the square represents how that stitch is to be worked.

Crochet

Single Crochet (sc) Edging

1 *Working from right to left, *insert crochet hook into a stitch at the edge of the fabric.*

2 *Yarn-over and pull the loop through the stitch, yarn-over and pull through both stitches on hook. Repeat from * for desired number of stitches. (Left-handers: work from left to right.)*

Single Crochet Decrease (dec sc)

1 *Working in sc, insert hook into the next stitch, yarn-over and pull up a loop.*

2 *Insert hook into the next stitch, yarn-over and pull up a loop (3 loops on hook), yarn-over and draw loop through all 3 loops on hook at once. 1 dec. made*

Color Knitting

Fair Isle

Fair Isle knitting refers to knitting with more than one color, which requires the yarns to be carried across the wrong side of the work. This is called "stranding" and is often referred to as "carrying the yarn." The yarns are usually stranded over a small repeat of no more than 3 or 4 sets.

Intarsia

Intarsia is a color-work technique used for blocks of color where it's more practical to work from separate balls of yarns or bobbins than to carry the yarns across, as in Fair Isle.

Care should be taken to carry the yarn across the back so that the fabric doesn't become too tight, or "pucker." It helps to spread the stitches out a little on the left-hand needle before stranding the new color across to keep the strand loose, enabling the fabric to lie flat. Always carry one yarn below the other; the strands should run parallel on the wrong side.

At each color change, bring the new yarn up from under the yarn just used and continue with the new color; this will "lock" the two yarns and prevent holes.

Fringe

Simple Fringe

*For each fringe, cut enough strands of yarn for half of the desired fullness of fringe and twice the desired length of fringe. Fold the strands in half, insert a crochet hook from back to front through the stitch, and pull the fold through to the back. Pull the ends through the fold, and pull to tighten. Repeat from * for each fringe. Trim fringe edges neatly to desired length.*

Knotted Fringe

*Work a Simple Fringe (cutting strands at least twice as long to allow for additional knotting) across the edge to be fringed. Then, *beginning at the right edge, take half of the strands from the first fringe and knot them together with half of the strands from the next fringe, continuing in this manner to the end. Return to the right edge, take the remaining half of the strands from the first fringe, and knot them together with half of the strands from the next fringe, continuing across to the end. Repeat from * as desired. Trim neatly to desired length.*

Knitting Abbreviations

approx	approximately	pat(s)	pattern(s)	wyif	bring yarn forward between needles to the front of work
beg	begin(ning)	pm	place marker(s)		
cm	centimeter	rem	remain(ing)	yd(s)	yard(s)
cn	cable needle	rep	repeat(s)	yo	yarn-over. Bring yarn forward between needles, then over right-hand needle into position to work the next stitch.
cont	continue(ing)	RH	right-hand		
dec	decrease	rnd	round		
est	established	RS	right side (that is, public side)		
g	gram(s)				
inc	increase	sc	single crochet		
k	knit	selv st	selvage stitch	*	repeat instructions after or between asterisks across row or round as instructed
k1-tbl	knit 1 stitch through the back loop	skp	slip 1 stitch knitwise from left-hand needle to right-hand needle; knit next stitch, then pass the slipped stitch over the stitch just knit, then off needle. This is a left-leaning decrease.		
				[ ]	repeat instructions with in brackets as instructed
k2tog	knit 2 stitches together as one, decreasing 1 stitch. This is a right-leaning decrease.				

Knit with Beads Abbreviations

BK1	knit 1 bead through a knit stitch
BP1	purl 1 bead through a purl stitch
Byo	slide 1 bead up to right-hand needle, then work a yarn-over in the usual way, holding bead in place on right side of work with thumb
HB1	hook 1 bead with crochet hook
SBU	slide bead up

k3tog	knit 3 stitches together as one, decreasing 2 stitches
LH	left-hand
m	meter(s)
M1	Make 1 increase. Increase by inserting left-hand needle under horizontal strand between stitch just worked and next stitch; knit strand through the back.
mm	millimeter(s)
mult	multiple
oz	ounce
p	purl
p1-tbl	purl 1 stitch through the back loop
p2tog-tbl	purl 2 stitches together as one, decreasing 1 stitch. This is a left-leaning decrease.

sk2p	slip 1 stitch knit wise, knit next 2 stitches together, then pass the slipped stitch over and off needle
sl st	slip stitch(es) as instructed
ssk	slip 2 stitches knit-wise one at a time from left-hand needle to right-hand needle; insert left-hand needle through fronts of these stitches and knit them together as one. This is a left-leaning decrease.
ssp	slip next 2 stitches one at a time as if to knit; pass stitches back to left-hand needle and p2tog-tbl
st(s)	stitch(s)
tog	together
WS	wrong side

Sources for Materials

My sincere gratitude to the following suppliers, who generously provided materials for the projects in this book.

Yarns

(These companies are wholesale only. Please contact them to locate yarn shops and craft stores in your area that carry their products.)

Berroco, Inc.
Elmdale Road
P.O. Box 367
Uxbridge, MA 01569
(508) 278-2527
www.berroco.com

Classic Elite Yarns, Inc.
122 Western Avenue
Lowell, MA 01851
(978) 453-2837
www.classiceliteyarns.com

Coats & Clark
Coats & Clark Moda-Dea
Consumer Services
P.O. Box 12229
Greenville, SC 29612-0229
(800) 648-1479
www.coatsandclark.com
www.modadea.com

Green Mountain Spinnery
P.O. Box 568
Putney, VT 05346
(800) 321-9665
www.spinnery.com

JCA Crafts, Inc.
(Artful Yarns Portrait and Reynolds Utopia)
35 Scales Lane
Townsend, MA 01469
(978) 597-8794
www.jcacrafts.com

Lion Brand Yarn Company
34 West 15th Street
New York, NY 10011
(212) 243-8995
www.lionbrand.com

Patons Yarns
320 Livingstone Avenue South
Listowel, Ontario N4W 3H3
Canada
(888) 368-8401
www.patonsyarns.com

Plymouth Yarn Company, Inc.
P.O. Box 28
Bristol, PA 19007
(215) 788-0459
www.plymouthyarn.com

Tahki–Stacy Charles, Inc.
P.O. Box 568
Ridgewood, NY 11385
(800) 338-yarn
www.tahkistacycharles.com

Westminster Fibers (Rowan)
4 Townsend Avenue, Unit 8
Nashua, NH 03063
(800) 445-9276
www.westminsterfibers.com
www.knitrowan.com

Beads

Lyden Enterprises, Home of The Beadwrangler
228 N. Sun Court
Tampa, FL 33613
(888) 235-0375
www.7beads.com
www.beadwrangler.com

Beads World, Inc.
1384 Broadway
New York, NY 10018
(212) 302-1199
www.beadsworldusa.com

Caravan Beads
326-A Nutt Street
Wilmington, NC 28401
(910) 343-0500
email: caravanbeads@bellsouth.net

Cartwright's Sequins
11108 N. Hwy. 348
Mountainburg, AR 72946
www.ccartwright.com

Wichelt Imports/Mill Hill
N162 Hwy. 35
Stoddard, WI 54658
www.wichelt.com
www.millhill.com

Notions

JHB International
1955 S. Quince Street
Denver, CO 80247
(800) 525-9007
www.buttons.com

Susan Bates
(steel crochet hook)
Distributed by Coats & Clark
See Coats & Clark

Bibliography

Allen, Pam, and Ann Budd. *Wrap Style.* Loveland, CO: Interweave Press, 2005.

Chin, Lily. *Knit and Crochet with Beads.* Loveland, CO: Interweave Press, 2004.

Davis, Jane. *Knitting with Beads.* New York: Lark Books, 2003.

Durant, Judith, and Jean Campbell. *The New Beader's Companion.* Loveland, CO: Interweave Press, 2005.

Hiatt, June Hemmons. *The Principles of Knitting.* New York: Simon and Schuster, 1989.

Rush, Hélène. *The Knitter's Design Sourcebook.* Camden, ME: Down East Books, 1991.

Stanley, Montse. *The Reader's Digest Guide to Knitting.* Pleasantville, NY: Reader's Digest, 1993.

Thomas, Mary. *Mary Thomas's Knitting Book.* London: Hodder and Stoughton, Ltd., 1943. Reprint. New York: Fireside, 2002.

Vogue Knitting: The Ultimate Knitting Book. New York: Pantheon Books, 1989.

Walker, Barbara G. *A Treasury of Knitting Patterns.* Pittsville, WI: Schoolhouse Press, 1998.

———. *A Second Treasury of Knitting Patterns.* Pittsville, WI: Schoolhouse Press, 1998.

Wiseman, Nancie M. *The Knitter's Book of Finishing Techniques.* Woodinville, WA: Martingale & Company, 2002.

Index

Beads
  basics 10
  pre-stringing 12
Big-eye needle 12
Bind-offs
  picot 26
  3-needle 90
Blocking and laundering 14

Cables 90
Cape, Double-breasted, with beaded trim 20
Capelets
  Bobbles and Beads 74
  Pearl 40
  Sapphire Dream 58
Casting on stitches with beads 13
Cast-ons
  knit-on 91
  long-tail 91
  picot 26
Charts 92

Crochet
  single crochet decrease 92
  single crochet edging 92

Fair Isle 93
Fringes
  knotted 93
  simple 93

Hook beading 68

Intarsia 93

Ponchini, Bows and Beads 70
Ponchos
  Beaded Tweed 30
  Southwestern 34

Sequins, knitting with 84
Shawls
  Enchanted 44
  Fireside 16

Spring Morn 64
Shawlette, Shimmering 86
Shrugs
  Nautical 48
  Sassy 24
Slip-stitch beaded knitting 38
Stitching beads to knitted fabric 78
Stole, Houndstooth 80

Techniques for knitting with beads
  between purl stitches 28
  hook beading 68
  in Garter stitch 15
  on a yarn-over 62
  slip-stitch beaded knitting 38
  through a knit stitch 52
  through a purl stitch 53

Wrap, Argyle 54

Yarns 10–11